Warrior • 87

Italian Arditi

Elite Assault Troops 1917–20

Angelo L Pirocchi • Illustrated by Velimir Vuksic

First published in Great Britain in 2004 by Osprey Publishing,
Midland House, West Way, Botley, Oxford OX2 0PH, UK
44-02 23rd St, Suite 219, Long Island City, NY 11101, USA
E-mail: info@ospreypublishing.com

© 2004 Osprey Publishing Ltd.

Transferred to digital print on demand 2010
First published 2004
1st impression 2004
Printed and bound by Cadmus Communications, USA

A CIP catalogue record for this book is available from the British Library

ISBN: 978 1 84176 686 7

Editorial by Ilios Publishing, Oxford, UK (www.iliospublishing.com)
Design by Ken Vail Graphic Design, Cambridge, UK
Index and proofreading by Bob Munro
Originated by The Electronic Page Company, Cwmbran, UK

Front Cover: Arditi at the Piave River, 1918.
(MGR3/1235)

Author's dedication
To my wonderful wife, the last victim of the Arditi.

Author's acknowledgements
I would like to thank the following people for their precious support: Arturo Ansaloni of the *Museo Memoriale della Libertà*, Marco Balbi, Pierpaolo Battistelli, Marco Bosco, Tiziano Berté of the *Museo Storico Italiano della Guerra, Rovereto*, Andrea Brambilla, Edoardo Buzzi, Mauro Caimi, Andrea Carlucci, Cesare Calamandrei, Ruggero Dal Molin, Massimo Di Martino, Gianfranco Favero, Alessandro Massignani, Alberto Menichetti, Franco Mesturini, Luca Pastori, Ruggero Pettinelli, Gabriella and Federico Peyrani, Alessandro Raspagni, Gino Rossato, Ettore Tosi Brandi, Andrea Saccoman, Camillo Zadra of the *Museo Storico Italiano della Guerra, Rovereto*, and the staff of *Museo Nazionale d'Artiglieria di Torino*, Ten.Col. Cimini, M.llo Capo Galletti and M.llo Capo Regis. Particular thanks go to Federico Cavallero, president of the Turin Section of FNAI, for his expertise and timely advice, to Francesco Fatutta for his kind and priceless cooperation and to Joe Elrod, for his indulgence and professionalism. Without the help of Giovanni Brambilla and Paolo Zaninelli, who researched and collaborated on the chapters on weapons, equipment, training and everyday life, this book could not have been completed. They have to be considered as co-authors.

Image credits
The following abbreviations relate to the photographic captions that appear in this work.
Arch.   *Archivio* (Archive)
Coll.   *Collezione* (Collection)
FNAI   Federazione Nazionale Arditi d'Italia
MGR   Museo Storico Italiano della Guerra (Italian Museum of the History of War), Rovereto, Italy
MNA   Museo Nazionale d'Artiglieria (National Artillery Museum), Turin, Italy

FOR A CATALOGUE OF ALL BOOKS PUBLISHED BY OSPREY MILITARY AND AVIATION PLEASE CONTACT:

Osprey Direct, c/o Random House Distribution Center, 400 Hahn Road, Westminster, MD 21157
Email: uscustomerservice@ospreypublishing.com

Osprey Direct, The Book Service Ltd, Distribution Centre, Colchester Road, Frating Green, Colchester, Essex, CO7 7DW
E-mail: customerservice@ospreypublishing.com

www.ospreypublishing.com

Table of rank

Italian	Abbreviation	Equivalent
Generale dell'Esercito	Gen.	Field Marshal
Tenente Generale – Capo di Stato Maggiore – in comando d'Armata – in comando di Corpo d'Armata – in comando di Divisione	Ten.Gen.	General (Chief of Staff, Army) Lieutenant-General (Army Corps, Division)
Maggiore Generale – in comando di Divisione – in comando de Brigata	Magg.Gen.	Major-General
Brigadiere Generale	Brig.Gen.	Brigadier
Colonnello	Col.	Colonel
Tenente colonnello	Ten.Col.	Lieutenant-General
Maggiore	Magg.	Major
Capitano	Cap.	Captain
Tenente	Ten.	Lieutenant
Sottotenente	S.Ten.	Second-Lieutenant
Aspirante	Asp.	Acting Second Lieutenant
Aiutante di Battaglia	Aiut.	Warrant Officer
Maresciallo – Maresciallo Maggiore – Maresciallo Capo – Maresciallo Ordinario	M.llo – M.llo Magg. – M.llo Capo – M.llo Ord.	NCOs
Sergente Maggiore	Serg.Magg.	Sergeant-Major
Sergente	Serg.	Sergeant
Caporal Maggiore	C.M.	Corporal
Caporale	C.le.	Lance-Corporal
Soldato	Sol.	Private

CONTENTS

ITALIAN ARDITI ELITE ASSAULT TROOPS 1917–20

INTRODUCTION

During World War I, the fighting along the Italian Front became entrenched, with the continuous stream of assaults leading only to stalemate. The subject of this book, the Ardito (literally an 'audacious man'), was conceived of as an elite form of soldier (akin to modern-day special forces) who, together with his parent Reparto d'Assalto (assault unit), would be able to break this impasse and bring victory to the Italian Royal Army. Despite the common belief that this new type of soldier was inspired solely by similar troops created by the German and Austro-Hungarian forces at the time (*Sturmtruppen*), the Ardito's mission was much larger in scope. In fact in World War I only the Italian Army employed Assault Divisions (later an Army Corps) in offensive actions along large areas of the front, with the aim of breaching the enemy's defences and attacking in depth, thus preparing the way for a general infantry advance.

The Arditi had special recruitment procedures, training, arms, uniforms, privileges and benefits. For the first time, an Italian soldier was given concentrated, specific training, both psychological and physical; the Ardito also received the best available equipment and enjoyed superior living conditions. In order to counter the high casualty rate, discipline was administered in a less orthodox way, and awards were widely given out. Particular attention was focused on camaraderie and attitude, in order to motivate the men and help them bear the psychological stress involved. The *esprit de corps* was very important, and survived the war. A great number of Arditi veterans participated in the *Impresa di Fiume* (the Italian occupation of the Dalmatian town of Fiume in September 1919, now Rijeka in Croatia) led by the poet and war hero Gabriele D'Annunzio, and many of them were in the first Fascist paramilitary units which four years after the end of World War I supported Mussolini's rise to power.

This political affiliation is one, if not the major, reason why there are so few written works on the Arditi. Another reason is the fact that the Reparti d'Assalto were not assigned to a central command or inspectorate, and therefore much official information was poorly recorded or sometimes lost altogether. A final reason is that Assault units changed designation numbers three times. At first (between July and October 1917) the number was an arbitrary designation made by each Army – as shown (confusingly) by the 1st, 2nd and 4th Armies each having a 'IV Reparto' unit. Next came an initial re-organisation at the beginning of January 1918. Finally, there was a definitive reorganisation in May 1918. In addition, designation numbers were written in Roman numerals, so mistakes often occurred in both official records and in

The Ardito's 10 commandments

1) Ardito! Your name means courage, force and loyalty; your mission is victory, at any cost. Be proud to show the whole world that nobody can resist the Italian soldier. Think of the jewels you are defending with your valour: the freedom of your families, the beauty of your country, the wealth of your nation. This will give you invincible strength.

2) To win, numbers and weapons do not count: above all, discipline and boldness are the sole values. Discipline is the most beautiful and the highest moral force; boldness is the cold, firm will to show the enemy your superiority, whenever and wherever.

3) Victory lies beyond the last enemy trench, to the rear; to reach it, use violence and cleverness, and do not care if during the assault some of the enemy remains beyond your reach. If the enemy surrounds you, then surround the enemy.

4) Always try to absorb what is happening on the battlefield, and rush to help comrades in danger. When you feel the situation is perilous, then throw yourself forward, and forward again.

5) When attacking, use your hand grenades and dagger, the true weapons of every Ardito. When defending the terrain you have won, use your rifle and your machine gun. Protect your machine guns if you want them to protect you. Cover the sound of the enemy's charge with that of your machine guns. Then you will see the charge fail and the enemy falling like cut wheat.

6) If you catch the enemy in the rear, throw him into terror and disorder; there, one courageous man is worth a hundred men, an Italian Ardito worth a thousand enemy soldiers.

7) The terror your enemy experiences before you is your best weapon; be sure to further your fame. Be fierce with the standing enemy, be generous with the falling one.

8) If you are wounded or missing, your duty is to give news to your unit and to try to reach your comrades at any cost.

9) Do not aspire to any other prize than the smile of the beautiful Italian women you defend with your courage. They will cover you with flowers and will bestow kisses on you when you return victorious, proud of your masculinity, oh beloved son of great Italy.

10) Run into battle! You are the best example of the genius of our people! The whole country is watching you during your bold attack!

Ten.Gen. Francesco Saverio Grazioli, Commander of Assault Army Corps, June 1918

personal memoirs. For the first time, thanks to the groundbreaking work of Francesco Fatutta, a complete and hopefully definitive reconstruction of all existing Reparti d'Assalto can be attempted.

THE ORIGINS AND DEPLOYMENT OF THE ARDITI

The Arditi were first organised as operative units in June 1917, by order of the Supreme Command and under the direction of Ten.Col. Giuseppe A. Bassi. However, this step was merely the culmination of much previous combat experience and experimentation, all of which was based upon a move away from the principles of static trench warfare. A key stage of this was the introduction of the special soldiers called Esploratori (or scouts). These troops had been recruited and trained by the Italian Army since 1914, and were organised at regimental level. Their mission was to seek out and secure passages through barbed-wire entanglements under cover of darkness or in poor visibility, carry out reconnaissance, report enemy positions, cover the flanks during attacks, and ambush enemy patrols.

As at 24 May 1915, the date of the outbreak of war in Italy, each infantry regiment and each Alpini (mountain troop) battalion had a platoon of Esploratori which contained four officers and 80–90 soldiers, plus bicycle-mounted orderlies and a supply section with mules, for long-distance actions. They were chosen for their skill and courage, and

A group of NCOs bearing the combat standards of several Reparti d'Assalto. No two men are alike in terms of their uniform or equipment. The two men on the right and the first on the left are 'Crimson Flames', indicated by their collar patches: one sports a red fez and the others the Bersaglieri cap badge with the cornet. Note also the red standards with the cornet they bear. (Courtesy of Cesare Calamandrei and Editoriale Olimpia, Florence, from *Storia dell'arma bianca italiana*.)

were well trained. They wore a special badge, consisting of a six-pointed star, which was worn on the left sleeve. However, after only a few weeks of war, the entrenchment of the front called for a rethinking of the Esploratore role. Only in the mountains did the distance between the lines allow the employment of Esploratori, who were also given a wider range of tasks, such as conducting limited attacks on opposing trenches, storming enemy outposts, and taking prisoners.

Regulations laid down by the Supreme Command (Comando Supremo) called for the creation of pioneer squads, formed from engineer personnel with riflemen as escorts. Their mission was the destruction of enemy barbed-wire entanglements and the opening of pathways for attacking troops. These units, officially known as 'Wire-cutter companies', were manned for the most part by volunteers, many of whom were Esploratori: they called themselves 'Death companies' though, because of the high rate of losses among their members. They were equipped with sapper's tools, gelatin explosives, and long and short wire-cutters; they also wore special helmets, body armour and shields, as well as stiff leather gloves and long leather boots, with metal protectors over the knees. This protective clothing was soon abandoned though, because of its restrictive weight and insufficient protection against bullets and shrapnel. These units were operative until the end of 1916, when large-calibre mortars were widely adopted as the principal means of destroying barbed-wire obstacles.

Following the Supreme Command's directives of June 1915, which required an 'offensive impulse to be given to operations', some volunteer units were allowed to act as independent Esploratori companies, and achieved limited success in different areas of the front. One of them was the Compagnia Esploratori Volontari Baseggio, which was active in Valsugana (north of Mount Ortigara). This unit is important because after the war its commander, Cap. Cristoforo Baseggio, claimed to be the 'father of the Arditi' for his innovations: he began to teach his men guerrilla techniques, based on surprise and speed, and with a special emphasis on the morale of his men. They were successful in several minor actions but were all but wiped out in April 1916 during the attack on Mount Osvaldo, and the unit was disbanded in May. In truth, Cap. Baseggio did nothing more than follow the standard practices of mountain warfare, as prescribed in all the regulations that appeared between 1903 and 1916.

During the long and bloody fighting of 1916, regulations were issued in order to deal with the problem of low morale throughout the Italian Army. This situation was caused by the stalemate on the Isonzo front and the unexpected and successful 'Punitive Offensive' (*Strafexpedition*) of the Austro-Hungarian Army, which almost achieved victory in the Pasubio sector. Most of the Supreme Command's directives dealt with prizes to be awarded to soldiers who, acting on personal initiative, succeeded in taking prisoners (based on the current 'price' list, dealt with on page 18) or capturing enemy weapons. To encourage such initiative, an honour badge was instituted on 15 July 1916 for the '*Militare ardito*' (audacious soldier): it featured the royal monogram 'VE' (the initials of King Vittorio Emanuele III) and the Savoy knot sewn in silver yarn, and was awarded to soldiers who volunteered for risky actions. This was the first time the word '*ardito*' officially appeared in Italian Army terminology, although the institution of the formal units was still some way off. In fact it was clearly emphasised that the 'VE' was a symbol of personal courage, an example to be followed by other members of the unit, and not a badge referring to a specific unit.

At the same time, many officers with extensive field experience were trying out innovative tactics in an attempt to break the deadlock of the opposing lines. Many drew inspiration from the intelligence briefing regarding the Austro-Hungarian stormtrooper, which was issued on 14 March 1917, as well as the latest tactical directives issued in January 1917. No change in any unit's order of battle was allowed: however, misinterpretation of the briefing document was partly responsible for the institution of the 'Arditi Regimental Platoon' in many regiments, a unit that was nonetheless confirmed in later regulations, and fostered after the creation of the Arditi units. For example, the 2nd and 3rd Armies ordered their Arditi regimental platoons to attend the Arditi training school, in order to absorb the latest tactical thinking.

One of the most open-minded officers was Cap. Giuseppe Bassi, whose proposal on the 'Institution and employment of sub-machine gun sections' of 8 November 1916 drew the attention of his brilliant superior, Brig.Gen. Francesco Saverio Grazioli. As a result, Bassi was authorised to train an experimental platoon of sub-machine gunners, while Grazioli ordered his brigade officers to experiment with specialist platoons, and also established a training area at Russig, near Gorizia. The first employment of the resultant tactical developments was the successful assault on Mount San Marco on 14 May 1917. The newly promoted Magg. Bassi was next ordered to organise a whole company to test out his ideas, which in the meantime had been extended to include the use of machine guns and other equipment, as well as new concepts of training and tactics. On 25 June 1917, the experimental company completed several exercises at Russig, with such a satisfactory result that the following day the Supreme Command ordered the institution of one Reparto d'Assalto for each Army. The Arditi had been born.

The only Army in a position to comply with the order was the 2nd Army, which on 10 July 1917 set up the first Arditi school and the I Reparto at Sdricca di Manzano, near Gorizia, under the command of the now Ten.Col. Bassi. He immediately designed a specific unit badge, and a more comfortable uniform. While the Supreme Command approved the badge, the new uniform was refused for being too civilian in appearance. Only when King Vittorio Emanuele III had visited the school on 29 July 1917 with the Chief of Staff and some foreign guests, one being the Prince of Wales, and judged the exercises as extremely well held, was the request for a new uniform and new equipment approved by the Supreme Command.

A young Ardito of 2nd Assault Divison: beneath his assault badge is the valour badge 'VE', earned before his enrolment in an assault unit. The badge is in black woollen yarn to better camouflage it. On his chest is the campaign ribbon for the 1915–18 war, also called the 'war efforts medal'. (Coll. Buzzi)

The 4th Army followed the example of the 2nd Army, and managed to form its first Reparto (the IV) at the end of July, while the 2nd Army began forming the II Reparto in August. On 10 August, the Supreme Command ordered the other Armies to send officers to Sdricca, with the specific task of being trained as instructors for their own units.

The baptism of fire for the I Reparto was on Mount Fratta, over the Isonzo River on 18 and 19 August 1917, during the eleventh Isonzo battle. Two companies of Arditi, under Ten.Col. Bassi's command, crossed the river, stormed the Austro-Hungarian front line and captured the crest of Mount Fratta. Five hundred prisoners, eight machine guns and two mortars were captured, while Italian losses were light. During the same period the I Reparto's 3rd Arditi company captured Belpoggio, near Gorizia. Both actions were a success, but were not fully exploited due to the late arrival of the regular infantry units.

The most renowned action, again with the King and foreign observers watching, was the capture of Mount San Gabriele on 4 September 1917: following a brief but concentrated artillery barrage, three companies of Arditi attacked the enemy lines, stormed the initial defences and cleared the trenches with hand grenades and flame-throwers, before repelling several counter-attacks. More than 3,000 prisoners, 55 machine guns and 26 trench guns were captured. Once again, success was limited by the late arrival of the infantry units, which had been hit heavily in their starting positions. Arditi losses were 61 killed and around 200 wounded, out of a total of 500 men.

Following the success of these impressive initial actions, the Supreme Command accelerated the formation of other Reparti. At the time of the tragic Italian defeat at Caporetto on 24 October 1917 there were approximately 20 units either operative or in training, and six units in the process of formation (see Table 1 on opposite page).

The units of the 2nd Army were widely employed as the rearguard of their retreating Army and consequently took heavy casualties. For example, the I Reparto was given the order to defend Udine at all costs, and here it suffered six officers and 385 men dead or wounded, while the remaining 70 were taken prisoner after running out of ammunition. Only the 1st Company was not involved, because it was deployed elsewhere. The other units, merged into a task force, continued to fight and helped gain time for the retreat that followed from the Tagliamento to the Piave rivers. The remnants of the six Reparti were the last Italian troops to leave the field and cross the Piave, before the bridges were blown. The other Reparti fought to cover the retreat of the remaining Armies, sometimes with high losses. On the 3rd Army's front, the XXII Reparto lost 700 men out of 800, while the XX arrived at the Piave River with 200 men. The V Reparto of the 4th Army lost one-third of its men on Mount Piana, during the diversionary attack of 21 October in Trentino, and ended the retreat with four officers and 70 soldiers.

Table 1: Assault Units 1917		
Army and school	Reparto d'Assalto (Assault Unit)	Date of creation
2nd Army Sdricca di Manzano	I (First)	5 July
	II (Second)	2 August
	III (Third)	September
	IV (Fourth)	September
	V (Fifth)	October
	VI (Sixth)	October
	X (Tenth)	October
	XI (Eleventh)	October
	XII (Twelfth)	October
	XIII (Thirteenth)	October
	XIV (Fourteenth)	October
	XV (Fifteenth)	October
3rd Army Borgnano	XIX (Nineteenth)	September/October
	XX (Twentieth)	September/October
	XXI (Twenty-first)	September/October
	XXII (Twenty-second)	September/October
4th Army Zortea	IV (Fourth)	July
	V (Fifth)	September
	VI (Sixth)	September
	VII (Seventh)	September
	VIII (Eighth)	September
1st Army (somewhere near Vicenza)	IV (Fourth)	July
	IX (Ninth)	September
	XXIV (Twenty-fourth)	September
Comando Zona Carnia (no available information about the school)	XVIII (Eighteenth)	August/September
3rd Army Corps (somewhere in Valcamonica)	XVII (Seventeenth)	August/September
Comando Truppe Altipiani (somewhere near Vicenza)	XVI (Sixteenth)	August/September

Sources for Table 1:

Giorgio Rochat, *Gli Arditi della Grande Guerra*, and Francesco Fatutta's ground-breaking *Contributo ad una storia delle Truppe d'Assalto*.

Notes for Table 1:

IV Rep. (4th Army) was soon disbanded to form the other four units. V Rep. (4th Army) was disbanded in December, due to the great losses incurred at Monte Piana and Monte Tomba: the survivors were sent to VI Rep. (4th Army), together with survivors of XVIII Rep.; VI Rep. (4th Army) became the famous IX Rep. with 9th CdA (Corpo d'Armata) in the reorganisation of June 1918.

IV and VI Rep. (2nd Army) and III and V Rep. were respectively merged into the I Rep. (2nd Army) and II Rep. (2nd Army), while excess personnel were enlisted into a new III Rep. (2nd Army) in January 1918. I and II Rep. became XX and XXII Rep. (with 20th and 22nd CdAs) in the reorganisation of June 1918.

X, XI, XII and XIII Rep. (2nd Army) were not operative before Caporetto. XIV and XV Rep. (2nd Army) were disbanded immediately and provided soldiers for I and II Rep. (2nd Army). X, XI, XII and XIII Rep. were disbanded on 5 December 1917, and provided soldiers for I and II Rep. (2nd Army). They were re-formed in January 1918, X Rep. in the 2nd Army, XI, XII and XIII Rep. in the 5th Army.

The 'Commission of Inquiry into the Retreat from the Isonzo River to the Piave River' accused the Arditi of pillage and looting, and Ten.Gen. Giardino gave evidence that more than 30 soldiers, many of them Arditi, were executed during the retreat as an example. It is possible that there was some truth in the accusations, and the discipline situation remained unsatisfactory until March or April of 1918, as noted in several directives from the Supreme Command and in the memoirs of Arditi officers. The six Reparti of the 2nd Army were among the few units to fight while withdrawing without disbanding, paying a high price in terms of blood and suffering. In addition, they were employed in a manner they had not been equipped or trained for, and they were used whenever necessary as a screen between advancing Austrian and German forces and the routed Italian units.

As a result of the heavy losses incurred, some of the units were disbanded at the beginning of December, or were merged into other

Table 2: Reparti d'Assalto at the beginning of 1918	
Army/Army Corps	**Reparti d'Assalto (Assault Units)**
1st Army	I, II, III, IV, IX, XVI, XXIII, XXIV
2nd Army	X, XVIII
3rd Army	XIX, XX, XXI, XXII
4th Army	V, VI, VII, VIII
5th Army	XI, XII, XIII
3rd Army Corps	XVII

Note: I and II were originally the I and II of 2nd Army; IV, IX and XXIV were originally the IV, IX and XXIV of 1st Army; XVI was originally the XVI of Comando Truppe Altipiani. The III, V, X, XI, XII, and XIII Reparti were new units reconstituted with the same number of the Reparti disbanded in December. XXIII was an entirely new unit. The XVIII Reparto was a new unit instituted in February.

Arditi of the 151st Infantry Regiment, Sassari Brigade, taking a rest from the fighting in Santa Lucia di Piave, October 1918. They have standard infantry equipment and weapons, but carry daggers and wear the open collar tunic, with the regimental red and white collar patches and the Ardito badge, as prescribed by regulations. (MGR 2/173)

existing units, while other Reparti were retired from the line to re-organise and rest. At the beginning of January, a report of the Supreme Command showed that there were currently 21 Reparti in existence, with one scheduled to be formed in February (see Table 2 on the left).

The designation numbers of the Reparti were re-assigned by the Supreme Command, without regard to the unit's previous assignment within an Army, in order to stress the autonomy of the units. The assignation to a particular Army now depended strictly on the availability of camps with training facilities.

Some Reparti were soon combat ready, and I, II, IV and XVI Reparti (now part of the 1st Army) took part in the bloody battle of the Three Mountains (Valbella, Col del Rosso and Col d'Echele) on 28/29 January 1918, with heavy losses to both the Arditi and the accompanying units (three infantry brigades, five Alpini battalions and three Bersaglieri regiments). Once again the action was poorly co-ordinated due to the combination of the different infantry, Arditi and artillery units.

During winter and spring of 1918, the Arditi were only called into action to preserve the lines, to counter-attack, or to conduct limited assaults. In March, the VIII Reparto fought several times on the Piave River (Fossalta); the XXIX Reparto attacked a fortified outpost at Marco (Trentino) in April and Mt. Zugna in May. The XXIII and XXVII Reparto counter-attacked following a few limited Austro-Hungarian raids in the Lower Piave sector in April and May, inflicting more than 2,000 casualties and taking some 1,000 prisoners. The V Reparto (III Reparto before 10 May) made several incursions in its sector (Trentino), and one of them became legendary: with only four men, Ten. Sabatini succeeded in taking Mt. Corno on 13 May 1918. The III Reparto (XVII Reparto before 10 May) captured some important positions, taking around 900 prisoners and several artillery guns, machine guns and equipment at Cima Presena (Tonale).

During spring 1918, the Supreme Command decided once again to re-organise the Arditi units. A Reparto was attached to each Army Corps, to form a reserve force tasked with leading attacks and counter-attacks. Some Reparti were sent or instituted abroad: the XIII (later the II) was transferred to France in April, followed by the XXXII in September, and the XVI was transferred to Albania, while the XXXV went to Macedonia. In March, Reparti d'Assalto di Marcia (Replacement Assault Units) were formed as replacement and training units for each Army. Some of them were also deployed

King Vittorio Emanuele III rewards an Ardito for his actions in June 1918 in the Lower Piave sector, during the inspection of the 1st Assault Division, on 21 August 1918. The tall officer in the background, with his arms crossed, is Ten.Gen. Francesco Saverio Grazioli, the Commander of the Assault Army Corps. (MGR 7/2787)

in combat, such as the I and the III. On 10 May a definitive designation took place, which once again changed the numbering of all existing Reparti.

The designations were not the only things to be changed: on 10 June, following months of research and consultation, the Supreme Command decided to form a whole Assault Army Corps, comprising an Assault Division (entitled 'A' Division) and the 6th Czech Division, under the command of Ten.Gen. Francesco Saverio Grazioli: interestingly, Ten.Col. Bassi was fiercely opposed to the changes, and was thus removed and sent to command an infantry regiment. The 'A' Division encadred nine existing Reparti, divided into three Assault Groups (1st Group – X, XX, V Reparti; 2nd Group – XII, XIII, XIV Reparti; 3rd Group – VIII, XXII, XXX Reparti), while new Reparti had to be formed in order to take their place, and these new units received the same number, plus the designation 'L' in Roman numerals. Many of these later units never entered operational service.

The last Austro-Hungarian offensive in June 1918 (akin to the *Kaiserschlacht* operation on the Western Front) was the first test for the new unit, which was employed to contain and counter-attack the dangerous enemy advance in the Lower Piave sector. Although sometimes outflanked, the Division achieved several minor tactical victories, but did not spearhead the projected counter-offensive and suffered severe losses (1,100 casualties out of 5,000 active troops), so many that it was necessary to bring the Reparti back to rally and re-organize. After the battle, the commander of the 3rd Army, the Duke of Aosta, admitted that it had been a mistake to throw the poorly amalgamated division into battle, without adequate preparation or strategic planning. Nevertheless, the Supreme Command judged the results as positive, and continued with the formation of the Assault Army Corps, substituting the Czech Division with another Assault Division, split into three other Assault Groups. The six Assault Groups were formed from two Reparti d'Assalto and one Bersaglieri battalion, so 'A' Division became 1st Assault Division and provided three Reparti (V, XIV

Four of the five heroes of Mt. Corno. Ten. Sabatini, second from the left, bears a Gold Valour Medal, while Serg. Degli Esposti (first on the left) and the two other Arditi sport Silver Valour Medals. On 13 May 1918, after a difficult climb in exposed terrain, the five men took the fortified mountain top alone, killing or taking prisoner 26 of the defenders, and resisting counter-attacks until the rest of their unit arrived. They have the number of their Reparto (V) stencilled on their helmets. Ten. Sabatini also displays the war promotion badge on his cuffs and a 'wound' stripe. (Arch. Mauro Caimi)

Table 3: Reparti d'Assalto June 1918		
Reparto d'Assalto		**Sub-unit**
Final designation	**Previous designation**	Corpo d'Armata (CdA) – Army Corps
I (First)	X (Tenth) 2nd Army*	1st CdA (4th Army), then (June) 2nd Assault Division
II (Second)	XIII (Thirteenth) 5th Army*	2nd CdA, in France from April
III (Third)	XVII (Seventeenth) 3rd Army Corps	3rd CdA (7th Army), in autumn 4th Army
V (Fifth)	III (Third) 2nd Army*	5th CdA (1st Army), then (June) 1st and (end of June) 2nd Assault Division
VI (Sixth)	VIII (Eighth) 4th Army	6th CdA (4th Army), then (June) 2nd Assault Division
VIII (Eighth)	XXII (Twenty-second) 3rd Army	8th CdA (8th Army), then (June) 1st Assault Division
IX (Ninth)	VI (Sixth) 4th Army	9th CdA (4th Army), in autumn 4th Army
X (Tenth)	XXIV (Twenty-fourth) 1st Army	10th CdA (1st Army), then (June) 1st Assault Division
XI (Eleventh)	XX (Twentieth) 3rd Army	11th CdA (3rd Army), in autumn 3rd Army
XII (Twelfth)	XI (Eleventh) 5th Army*	12th CdA (6th Army), then (June) 1st Assault Division
XIII (Thirteenth)	XXI (Twenty-first) 3rd Army	13th CdA (6th Army), then (June) 1st Assault Division
XIV (Fourteenth)	XII (Twelfth) 5th Army*	14th CdA (6th Army), then (June) 1st and (end of June) 2nd Assault Division
XVI (Sixteenth)	–	16th CdA, in Albania
XVIII (Eighteenth)	IX (Ninth) 1st Army	18th CdA (4th Army), in autumn 4th Army
XX (Twentieth)	I (First) 2nd Army	20th CdA (6th Army), then (June) 1st Assault Division
XXII (Twenty-second)	II (Second) 2nd Army	22th CdA (9th Army), then (June) 1st Assault Division
XXIII (Twenty-third)	XIX (Nineteenth) 3rd Army	23th CdA (3rd Army), in autumn 4th Army
XXV (Twenty-fifth)	XVI (Sixteenth) Comando Altipiani	25th CdA (9th Army), then (June) 2nd Assault Division
XXVI (Twenty-sixth)	IV (Fourth) 1st Army	26th CdA (9th Army), in autumn 3rd Army
XXVII (Twenty-seventh)	V (Fifth) 4th Army*	27th CdA (8th Army), in autumn 8th Army
XXVIII (Twenty-eighth)	XVIII (Eighteenth) 2nd Army*	28th CdA (3rd Army), in autumn 3rd Army
XXIX (Twenty-ninth)	XXIII (Twenty-third) 1st Army*	29th CdA (1st Army), in autumn 1st Army
XXX (Thirtieth)	VII (Seventh) 4th Army	30th CdA (9th Army), then (June) 1st and (end of June) 2nd Assault Division
XXXI (Thirty-first)	–	1st Army
XXXII (Thirty-second)	–	From September in France with 2nd CdA
XXXV (Thirty-fifth)	–	From March, 35th Inf. Div. in Macedonia
LI (Fifty-first)	–	Created end of June under 1st CdA, but never completed
LII (Fifty-second)	–	52nd Mountain Div. (20th CdA, 6th Army), in autumn 6th Army
LV (Fifty-fifth)	–	5th CdA (1st Army), then in autumn 4th Army
LXX (Seventieth)	–	20th CdA (6th Army), then in autumn 6th Army
LXXII (Seventy-second)	–	22th CdA (9th Army), then in autumn 8th Army
LVIII (Fifty-eighth)	–	Created end of June under 8th, 10th, 12th, 13th, 14th and 30th CdAs, but soon disbanded. The personnel were transferred to the X and XI Reparti d'Assalto di Marcia (troops from LXXX were merged into LXXII Reparto).
LX (Sixtieth)	–	
LXII (Sixty-second)	–	
LXIII (Sixty-third)	–	
LXIV (Sixty-fourth)	–	
LXXX (Eightieth)	–	
I Reparto d'Assalto di Marcia (1st Replacement Assault Unit)		1st Army
II Reparto d'Assalto di Marcia (2nd Replacement Assault Unit)		2nd Army, then 8th Army
III Reparto d'Assalto di Marcia (3rd Replacement Assault Unit)		3rd Army
IV Reparto d'Assalto di Marcia (4th Replacement Assault Unit)		4th Army
V Reparto d'Assalto di Marcia (5th Replacement Assault Unit)		5th Army, then 9th Army
VI Reparto d'Assalto di Marcia (6th Replacement Assault Unit)		6th Army
VII Reparto d'Assalto di Marcia (7th Replacement Assault Unit)		7th Army

(continued top of page 13)

Reparto d'Assalto di Marcia 'A' ('A' Replacement Assault Unit); then X Reparto d'Assalto di Marcia (10th Replacement Assault Unit)	Assault Army Corps, 1st Division
XI Reparto d'Assalto di Marcia (11th Replacement Assault Unit)	Assault Army Corps, 2nd Division

and XXX) to the 2nd Assault Division, which also received troops from their Army Corps' I, VI and XXV Reparti. The Bersaglieri battalions, in Grazioli's mind, were perfect for providing a more powerful (with regard to the Arditi) and quicker (with regard to the regular infantry) force to man and defend the captured trenches after the first successful attack.

During the Austro-Hungarian offensive, the other Reparti fought fiercely along the whole front, opposing diversionary or secondary attacks, some of which were extremely dangerous. In the Mt. Grappa sector, the IX Reparto, on three separate days, recaptured Mt. Fagheron, Mt. Fenilon and the Col Moschin. The assault on the Col Moschin is often considered the Arditi's most successful action, with them taking the mountain in just 10 minutes with few losses while capturing 400 or so prisoners. Ten days later, the same unit took Mt. Asolone, losing 19 officers and 305 men. On Montello, the XXVII Reparto resisted for four days and was the mainstay of the defence, losing a quarter of its men. On the Piave River, near the positions of 'A' Division, the XXIII and XXVIII Reparti ended the engagement with 100 and 200 men respectively.

After the battle, some Reparti were employed to consolidate the front line and to harass the enemy, in order to maintain the initiative and prepare for the upcoming Italian offensive. During this period, while the Assault Army Corps was training vigorously, other Arditi Reparti took part in numerous unsuccessful operations, which seemed to damage their image. In effect, the post-combat reports often state that Arditi were employed without the necessary preparation and without the surprise factor, sometimes due to poor orders by higher command, sometimes due to the naivety of the officers who led them, who sacrificed technical proficiency for an overzealous faith in success. Additionally, initial successes often turned into withdrawals as units ran out of ammunition and were exposed to enemy counter-attacks.

The independent Reparti met with the same poor results during the great Italian offensive of 24 October 1918, principally because the enemy was well prepared for the assault. For example, the famous IX

Notes:
* Reparti instituted in January 1918, or in February (the XVIII). The other ones were already in existence in 1917: the ones not indicated were formed in May/June 1918. The Reparti di Marcia were formed in March 1918.
The following Reparti wore crimson-flame patches: XXIII, XXVI, LXXII.
The following Reparti wore the green-flame patches: III, XXIX, XXXI, LII.
The following had companies wearing black, green and crimson flames: VI, XXX, IV Reparti d'Assalto di Marcia.
The following Reparti d'Assalto di Marcia wore black-flame patches (2 coys) and crimson-flame patches (1 coy): II, III.
The following Reparto d'Assalto di Marcia wore black-flame patches (2 coys) and green-flame patches (1 coy): XI.
The remaining Reparti wore black-flame patches.

Arditi of the 1st Assault Division parade bare chested in front of the King to show off their strength. As far as we know, it was the first (and probably the last) time that such behaviour was permitted in the history of the Italian Army. (MGR 40/8)

Reparto lost 28 officers and 410 men out of a force of 30 officers and 500 men. In two days of fierce fighting on the Col della Berretta, it also lost the replacements received on the second day of the offensive. The LV and XXIII captured and lost Mt. Prasolan several times and were unable to capture Mt. Asolone. The III Reparto was halted for three days on Mt. Solaroli and captured and lost Mt. Cucco. The XVIII took Mt. Pertica but was halted there. The plan nevertheless succeeded, as the enemy diverted many divisions in order to reinforce the Grappa sector. On the Piave River, only the retreat of the enemy saved the XXVIII Reparto from total destruction (only one officer survived the battle), while the XI crossed the Piave River and defended the bridgehead near Grave di Papadopoli (in the Lower Piave) for four days. In other sectors, the Arditi encountered a weakened enemy, and the XXIX Reparto easily

---

Table 4: Assault Army Corps, end of June 1918
Commander: Ten.Gen. Francesco Saverio Grazioli

Army Corps troops
General Staff, Logistics Offices
Chemical Section
162nd Carabinieri Section (MP)
54th Motorised Section
73rd Signal Company
12th Searchlight Section
'A' Assault Replacement Unit
(in October: 10th Assault Repl. Unit, 11th Assault Repl. Unit and Bersaglieri Repl. Unit)

1st Assault Division	2nd Assault Division
Commander: Gen.Div. Ottavio Zoppi	*Commander: Gen.Div. Ernesto De Marchi*
227th and 365th Carabinieri Platoons (MP)	406th and 409th Carabinieri Platoons (MP)
16th Motorised Section	19th Motorised Section
1769th, 1770th and 178th Machine-gun Companies	317th, 279th and 589th Machine-gun Companies
3rd Bersaglieri Ciclisti (Cycle) Battalion	11th Bersaglieri Ciclisti (Cycle) Battalion
5th Squadron Cavalleggeri di Piacenza (Cavalry)	6th Squadron Cavalleggeri di Piacenza (Cavalry)
1st Assault Regroupment:	*2nd Assault Regroupment:*
1st Assault Group (X and XX Assault Units, 1st Bersaglieri Battalion)	4th Assault Group (XIV and XXV Assault Units, 3rd Bersaglieri Battalion)
2nd Assault Group (XII and XIII Assault Units, 7th Bersaglieri Battalion)	5th Assault Group (I and V Assault Units, 15th Bersaglieri Battalion)
3rd Assault Group (XXII and VIII Assault Units, 9th Bersaglieri Battalion)	6th Assault Group (VI and XXX Assault Units, 55th Bersaglieri Battalion)
9th Mountain Artillery Battalion	12th Mountain Artillery Battalion
91st Engineer Battalion	92nd Engineer Battalion
122nd Signal Company	71st Signal Company
70th Medical Section	86th Medical Section
75th Logistics Section	65th Logistics Section
14th Motorised Section	17th Motorised Section

Independent Reparti d'Assalto, autumn 1918	
Army/Army Corps/Division	**Reparti d'Assalto**
1st Army	XXIX, XXXI (I Reparto di Marcia)
3rd Army	XI, XXVI, XXVIII (III Reparto di Marcia)
4th Army	III, IX, XVIII, XXIII, LV (IV Reparto di Marcia)
6th Army	LII, LXX (VI Reparto di Marcia)
7th Army	(VII Reparto di Marcia)
8th Army	XXVII, LXXII (II Reparto di Marcia)
9th Army	(V Reparto di Marcia)
2nd Army Corps (France)	II, XXXII
16th Army Corps (Albania)	XVI
35th Infantry Division (Macedonia)	XXXV

(ABOVE) **Note:** During the battle of Vittorio Veneto (24 October 1918 – 4 November 1918), two Mountain Artillery Groups were added to the two Assault Regroupments (44th Mountain Artillery Battalion and 29th Mountain Artillery Battalion respectively), and one Machine-gun Company was given to each Bersaglieri Battalion.

(LEFT) **Note:** It is possible that V and VII Reparti di Marcia were disbanded, their Army being without any Assault Unit.

entered Rovereto and Trento; after 30 October the II and LXX met little resistance save rearguard actions in Trentino.

The Assault Army Corps' task was to attack in two different directions in order to cut the enemy's front in two. The 1st Division attacked to the north of Montello and the 2nd Division to the south of it: the latter was stopped by the flooding of the Piave River (which destroyed several bridges) and the former by enemy resistance, which inflicted severe losses on the advancing units. Only on 29 October did the 2nd Division cross the river, threatening the rear of the resisting Austro-Hungarian units, and capturing the important communication centre of Vittorio Veneto. After 31 October, the attack turned to pursuit along the whole front, and the Assault Army Corps led the advance on Cadore, where the end of the war on 4 November halted the Arditi's efforts. In ten days, they had lost 336 men (of which 18 were officers), with 56 men missing in action, and had more than 980 wounded, while capturing approximately 8,000 prisoners, 68 guns and 223 machine guns.

CHRONOLOGY OF THE WAR ON THE ITALIAN FRONT

1915

26 April Treaty of London: the Kingdom of Italy, formally allied with the Central Powers (Germany and Austria-Hungary), agrees with the Entente Powers to enter the war on their side, in return for territorial gains in the Italian Peninsular and the colonies.

24 May Italy declares war on the Austro-Hungarian Empire. Gen. Cadorna is the Italian Army Chief of Staff, Salandra is Prime Minister, and (formally) King Vittorio Emanuele III is the Supreme Commander of the Italian Armed Forces.

23 June–7 July First Battle of the Isonzo River. Cadorna's bloody and pointless strategy, based on the offensive at any cost, is executed and gains the Italian Army a small advance (about 25km) in all sectors. The front forms a large horizontal 'S', from the Stelvio Pass (on the border with Switzerland), to the Adriatic Sea, taking in the peaks of Adamello, Ortles, and Cevedale, Lake Garda, then Pasubio, the Asiago Plains, Mount Grappa, Cadore, the Alps of Carnia, and the Isonzo River, mostly following the old 1866 border. The order of battle is: 1st Army in Trentino, 4th Army in Cadore, 2nd Army from Cadore to Gorizia, 3rd Army from Gorizia to the sea.

18 July–3 August Second Battle of the Isonzo River. Italian troops take Mount San Michele. Both armies start to dig in. Hopes for a swift war dissolve.

18 October–5 December Third and Fourth battles of the Isonzo River. The Italian Army takes severe losses to gain only a few hundred metres in the infamous 'Cadorna shoulder push'.

December 1915–January 1916 The Italian Royal Navy rescues the remains of the Serbian Army.

The situation on the Italian front the day before Caporetto. The front followed the original border, except for the limited Italian conquests (marked in plain grey) and for the terrain lost during the *Strafexpedition* of 1916 (marked in lined grey). (G. Peyrani)

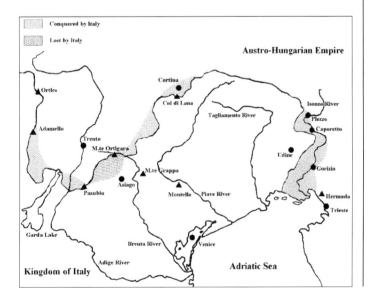

1916

11–29 March Fifth Battle of the Isonzo River: agreement with the Allies to reduce the pressure on the Western Front. Cadorna's strategy changes, preferring localised superiority of men and artillery to broader attacks along large sections of the front.

15 May–15 June The *Strafexpedition*, an Austro-Hungarian punitive offensive, inflicts the first territorial losses on the Italians. The Austro-Hungarian vanguards reach the Veneto plains, before being halted.

10 June Salandra resigns: the new Prime Minister is Paolo Boselli.

15 June–15 July Italian counter-offensive takes place on the Asiago Plains.

4–17 August Sixth Battle of the Isonzo River takes place.

9 August The first major Italian victory: the Italian Army takes Gorizia.

25 August Italy declares war on Germany.

14 September–1 November Seventh, Eighth and Ninth battles of the Isonzo River. The new Austro-Hungarian Emperor Charles I names Arz von Straussenburg as Chief of Staff to replace Conrad von Hoetzendorf.

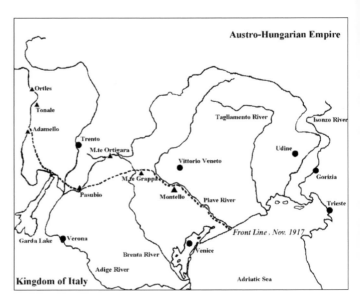

1917

12 May–6 June Tenth Battle of the Isonzo River, following the Chantilly Conference. The losses are enormous: 160,000 Italians and 90,000 Austro-Hungarians. The Italian 3rd Army's artillery fires more than a million rounds in one day – one round on each 1.5cm of the front.

10–29 June The Battle of Mount Ortigara, also known as 'the Alpini's calvary'.

5 July The first Reparto d'Assalto is instituted within the 2nd Army.

18 August–12 September Eleventh Battle of the Isonzo River, the Italians take the Bainsizza Plains. The Arditi fight their first battle, on Mt. Fratta.

4 September The battle of Mt. San Gabriele: the Arditi take 3,127 prisoners.

24 October–9 November An Austro-Hungarian and German force, following a gas bombardment, breaks through the Italian lines, and the Caporetto retreat begins. The Italian Army loses one-third of its manpower, thousands of artillery pieces and carriages, a large amount of ammunition and numerous supply depots. The Arditi fight as a rearguard force and ensure that the routed troops reach the last line of defence, on the Piave River.

26 October Boselli resigns: Vittorio Emanuele Orlando takes over as Prime Minister.

8 November Gen. Cadorna is replaced by Gen. Armando Diaz as Chief of Staff, with Gen. Badoglio and Gen. Giardino as adjutants.

10 November–26 December The Italian Army halts the Austro-German offensive across the entire front.

1918

January 1918 A limited counter-offensive on the Asiago Plains takes place, and the lines are rectificied along the front. Recruits of the class of 1899 receive their baptism of fire in the Piave River sector. The Arditi fight in the Battle of the Three Mountains (28/29 January).

January–May The Italian Army begins a programme of rebuilding and improvement. An English and a French Division arrive on the Italian Front. The Arditi conduct an exemplary action at Monte Corno (13 May).

10 June The Assault Army Corps is formed.

15 June–6 July The last Austro-Hungarian offensive on the Piave River, Mt. Grappa and the Asiago Plains ('Battle of Solstice'). After initial successes, the

The disastrous situation facing Italy on 10 November 1917, in the aftermath of Caporetto. The Austro-German offensive also overwhelmed the second Italian defensive line on the Tagliamento River, and the Italian Army fought hard to stop the advance at the Piave River. (G. Peyrani)

advancing troops are halted and sent back to their starting positions. 1st Arditi Division is sacrificed on the Piave; IX Reparto achieves its famous victory on the Col Moschin and Mt. Asolone (Mt. Grappa).

24 October One year after Caporetto, the Italian Army, with the support of English and French troops, begins the final battle of Vittorio Veneto. All Arditi units take part in the fighting, and lead the way.

29 October Austro-Hungary offers its unconditional surrender.

3 November The armistice of Villa Giusti. Italian troops enter Trento and Trieste.

4 November The war ends on the Italian front. Italy has lost 578,000 men, compared to Austro-Hungarian losses of 1,100,000.

RECRUITMENT

In peacetime, all 18-year-old males, excluding the disabled or those with special family circumstances (such as fathers without wives, or the only sons of widowed mothers), were supposed to serve for two years. Each class was based on the age of the recruits; the class of 1899, for example, took in all males born in that year. The class was divided into four categories, which were based on the recruit's physical ability or family circumstances. The first category (comprising single, childless men in good health) of the first eight classes formed the Regular Army (*Esercito Permanente*), while the first category of the following four classes formed the Reserve Army (*Milizia Mobile*). The remaining seven classes, with its first, second and third categories and the third category of the other 12 classes, formed the Home Guard (*Milizia Territoriale*). Replacements were taken from the second category of the first 12 classes, respectively. The fourth category comprised those who were exempt from service.

Nineteen age classes were called for enlistment into the Army's ranks from 1881 to 1900 (the enlistment year for the latter being 1918). In total, more than five million Italian males were enlisted, from a population in 1915 of about 32.5 million people. In wartime, the Regular Army numbered between 1,000,000 in 1916 and 2,100,000 men in 1918.

With the draft system in use, only a small part of the Army structure consisted of professional soldiers. Most of the middle or higher-ranking

The officers of the famous IX Reparto after the successful attack on the Col Moschin in June 1918. The officer in the centre left with the cane is the commander, Magg. Giovanni Messe, later Marshal of Italy in World War II. The officer next to him with the Alpino hat is Cap. Angelo Zancanaro: he was awarded the Silver Valour Medal in World War I and the Gold Valour Medal in World War II. Most of the other young officers did not survive the war. In the background, a soldier sports a captured M16 Austro-Hungarian helmet. (Arch. Andrea Brambilla)

A group of Bersaglieri and Arditi of V and XXX Reparti, in May 1918, after the conquest of Mt. Corno, for which they have received awards. Awards were granted only for outstanding bravery. (Arch. Mauro Caimi)

officers were career soldiers and, as in the other European armies, were noblemen or came from the upper-middle class (being sons of business and industry proprietors, or the upper echelons of civil administration). Only a small number of NCOs were professional soldiers: most of them were assigned to the logistics branch, and wished to become rich at the expense of the Army. There was a complete lack of a professional and conscientious class of NCOs, well trained and efficient, to whom the responsibility of leading and training the soldiers could be passed. These duties were typically performed by a limited number of young professional officers, but only because it was a necessary step to forward their careers; subsequently, they had no interest in creating and maintaining good relationships with their men. Cultural differences, especially between officers and enlisted men, were widespread, and in a country where a large part of the population lived in the countryside and had little or no education, they were almost insuperable.

Due to the great wartime need for NCOs and low-ranking officers to lead the troops, a large number of complement officers, educated in brief and incomplete training courses, were employed; some troops were also promoted from the ranks to positions of minimal responsibility.

Since the Arditi were recruited from other Italian Army units, they represented a perfect cross-section of Italian society. One of the best sources on the Arditi, Salvatore Farina, an officer of the I Reparto, states that more than half of the Arditi were peasants, 30 per cent were factory workers and the remaining 20 per cent held 'other jobs'.

Initially, Arditi officers visited other infantry units and encouraged volunteers to come forward by highlighting the privileges on offer. An Ardito received 20 cents extra pay above the standard soldier's pay of 10 cents; a corporal's pay was 20 cents above the standard 25, and a sergeant's was 30 cents above the standard 1 lira and 88 cents. NCOs were paid between 1 lira and 2 lire and 50 cents, depending on rank. A soldier's pay was actually 89 cents, but there were deductions for food (38 cents), for clothing (14 cents) and bread (27 cents). All troops in a combat area received a war allowance of 40 cents.

Due to the special nature of the Ardito's role, spearheading the attack, they were often more successful than regular infantrymen in taking prisoners and capturing enemy *matériel*. According to the 1916 regulations, the rewards for taking a prisoner were 10 lire for a private, 20 lire for an NCO, and 50 lire for an officer. Capturing an enemy rifle entitled the soldier to 5 lire, a machine gun to 50 lire, and an artillery piece to 500 lire. Initially, these rewards were only given when such action demonstrated individual initiative, and not during operations ordered by command. By the end of the war, however, rewards were usually paid for any captured *matériel*.

The following figures provide some sort of comparison between the levels of pay and reward, and daily living costs. In 1917, a kilo of bread cost 55 cents, a kilo of pasta 89 cents, a kilo of potatoes 39 cents, a kilo of meat 3 lire and 74 cents, a cigar 17 cents, 10 cigarettes 36 cents, a postcard 5 cents, a litre of wine 1 lira and 20 cents, and a kilo of sugar 3 lire and 18 cents. A pair of shoes cost 34 lire and 70 cents – three times as much as in 1915.

The Ardito's daily food ration was better and more plentiful than the average soldier's. An Ardito was entitled to 230g of meat (compared to the 200g standard ration), 250g of rice or pasta (vs. 200g), and 700g of bread: he also received a daily ration of wine ($^1/_4$ litre) and coffee (10g), as opposed to the 70 rations per year of wine and 180 rations per year of coffee given to regular troops. Moreover, the Arditi's food was served hot, regularly and in a mess facility – quite different from the normally cold meal eaten in a muddy trench when the weather and the enemy permitted. After Caporetto, however, combat-troop meat rations were increased by 100g, and a wine ration was given daily, to encourage the shattered troops: the Arditi maintained their extra rations.

The Arditi jealously guarded their preferential treatment. One lieutenant reported how, after eating rice for days on end, the Arditi protested to the chaplain and demanded pasta. The priest promised to bring pasta for dinner, but when the Arditi discovered he had failed to do so, they emptied their mess tins and the large cooking pots on the grass, and forced the chaplain (an officer of the Italian Army) to sit in the rice and tomatoes, without his trousers. As proof of Christian charity, the chaplain never revealed the names of his tormentors.

Particular attention was given to permits for general leave, which were granted to the whole unit (or the relatively few survivors) after an operation. The distribution of awards was limited as it was difficult to single out exemplary actions. In fact, a surprisingly low number of the higher decorations were awarded, when one considers the number of successful operations and the outstanding bravery of the Arditi. Nevertheless, one Reparto earned the Gold Valour Medal as a unit, and several Reparti earned the next highest award, the Silver Valour Medal. Many Arditi (mostly officers) received Gold or Silver Valour Medals, but they made up only a small part of the total number awarded in the Italian Army.

The Arditi enjoyed other privileges too. They were exempt from camp chores such as guard duty, and avoided having to march (they were moved to the battle area in lorries) and carry backpacks. When the commander of the Assault Army Corps introduced the Ardito's pack, he had to issue the order several times, knowing that it was very unpopular. In addition,

An Arditi camp in the aftermath of the fighting in the Lower Piave, June 1918. The distribution of rations is taking place. The 'casse di cottura' or camp cookers were the standard cooking system in the Italian Army. After cooking, they could be filled with hot water, which would keep the food warm for several hours. (MGR 3/1231)

A group of 'Green Flames', Stokes section. Most of them wear the Alpini hat with the original cap badge (an eagle over two crossed rifles and a cornet). The Sottotenente in the centre has the Arditi machine-sewn badge on his hat, and displays Mountain Artillery collar patches on his closed collar. The rounds that the men are holding for the mortar are the British time-fused ones. (Arch. Marco Balbi)

the Arditi trained every day, unlike the regular infantry, who had no training at all save the drills for marching and shooting: the Arditi were not kept at the front, but were located in the rear, awaiting the call to action. They were exempt from trench duty, so as not to squander their training on boring and dangerous tasks.

In spite of the incentives on offer, when the newly formed first units of the 2nd Army began to experience high losses after the initial attacks, the number of volunteers began to decrease dramatically, falling from 50 to 20 per cent (and at one point even reaching 10 per cent). Only after Caporetto, with the enrolment of the last class (the 'boys of '99') and the widespread press attention on the Arditi, did the number of volunteers begin to rise. Thus the commanders of regular infantry regiments designated soldiers and NCOs from their own rolls to become Arditi: this was in fact the main source of recruitment, even though many memoirs focus on the voluntary side.

For each Arditi unit to be formed, each Army Corps regiment had to supply 10–15 soldiers and one or two corporals. Each brigade sent two corporals or sergeants and the divisions had to provide some NCOs. The selection criteria focused on the physical and military skills of the soldier, and paid particular attention to prior conduct and the individual's psychological state. The future Ardito had to be astute and courageous, physically and mentally strong, aggressive but disciplined, and whenever possible he should possess combat experience. He also had to be unmarried. The power to choose candidates allowed the regular-infantry officers to let the worst soldiers go, and keep the best soldiers in their units. Magg. Freguglia, commander of the XXVII Reparto, noted with some displeasure: 'Some infantry units have sent us the worst elements, leading these men to believe that becoming an Ardito would mean a life filled with all manner of comforts, higher pay, longer leave, relaxed discipline, and infrequent training'. To counter this problem, the training at the Arditi School was considered crucial, and specific tests to screen the candidates were introduced during training. When candidates did not meet the requirements, they were immediately returned to their previous units.

The common notion that the Arditi were criminals, 'dedicated to murder or to robbery', had no real basis in fact. In 1917, the Supreme Command issued a decree that strictly forbade the recruitment of common criminals into assault units. However, it is perfectly possible that soldiers were given the opportunity to enlist as volunteers in the Arditi in lieu of punishment for minor military misdemeanours. In the Italian Army of 1917–18, some 360,000 soldiers were prosecuted for many different reasons ranging from minor infringements to more serious crimes (excluding those sentenced to death for desertion, mutiny, or treason). After being sentenced the men returned to their units, while the punishment was suspended until the end of the war. So we can see that some Arditi will have had dealings with military justice, just like other soldiers in the Army. The Arditi themselves were proud of such rumours, as shown by the words to one of their songs:

> In the prisons there are no bandits
> They all went into the Arditi units
> If one has a six-year sentence he can be a corporal
> If another has a life sentence, he can be a general!

The officers were enlisted on a strictly voluntary basis. Incentives and privileges that might have enticed enlisted men to enrol were of no benefit to the officers: they did not earn any extra pay, they already ate better than the troops, were already exempt from fatigues, and had an orderly to take care of their necessities and to carry their property. So it is reasonable to assume that officers were motivated by idealistic reasons and by the desire to get away from trench routine. The prospect of belonging to an elite group, the cream of Italian officers, was an important factor as well. This sense of being an elite was transmitted to subordinate personnel through the choice of insignia, weapons and uniforms, by the development of the Ardito myth, along with the close interest in the soldiers' welfare.

Selection of the officers was even tougher than that of the enlisted men: they underwent the same screening tests as the troops, but in addition their command style was scrutinised, their morals and common sense were judged, and their ability to make decisions under severe stress and personal risk was checked. The evaluators sought out those men who would serve as an example for the others.

TRAINING

Once the applications of the draftees or volunteers had been processed, the Arditi candidates mustered at an Arditi school, the first and most famous being at Sdricca di Manzano, a small town near Gorizia, on the Natisone River. The other Arditi schools during this initial period were similar to this one, or rather, were closely modelled on this one. The visiting officers coming from other armies took away with them from Sdricca the training activities in use and installed them in the other schools. After Caporetto, Sdricca's officers conducted the training of new Arditi units in order to maintain the same proven standards, but there was no central school or an Army Corps school.

The new recruits were enrolled, and were then issued the new uniforms with the open tunic. However, they were not allowed to wear the black-flame collar patches, as these were only presented after one week's training. Nor were they allowed to wear the Ardito badge: they

A Reparto parades during the royal inspection of 1st Assault Division on 21 August 1918. From their movements, it seems that the Arditi are running, so this could be a 'Crimson Flame' unit, who, as Bersaglieri, usually ran instead of marching. (MGR 7/2788)

Arditi of XIII Reparto practise grenade-throwing exercises in Borso del Grappa, spring 1918. The smoke from the explosion of incendiary grenades provides cover for the attacking paired-up soldiers. The smoke also simulates gas attack, which would unsettle the defenders further. (Coll. Dal Molin)

would only be able to sew this on their left sleeve at the end of the course, and before then lay 15–20 days of hard work.

The first days were taken up with the physical and psychological admission tests, and with learning weapons basics, hand-grenade and dagger skills. A medical check-up was not considered, because the recruits already came from other Italian Army units. In order to weed out unfit and unsuitable soldiers, empirical tests had been developed by Arditi officers, along with physical tests in order to measure stamina and well-being. The most common one consisted of trained Arditi (called *nonni* or 'grandfathers' in army slang) throwing hand grenades at the candidates. The new recruits were taken to the hand-grenade range, and after a shout of 'attention', a whistle was blown: this was the signal for the *nonni* to throw the Thevenot. The candidate's behaviour while waiting and his reaction to the explosions gave the officers an insight into his psychological state and possible behaviour under the stress of combat.

In order to test their resistance to prolonged fire and risk exposure, the recruits were shut in a bunker, while the trainers threw grenades at the roof and at the entrance for extended periods. Incidentally, one of the worst mutinies of World War I on the Italian Front was caused by a similar situation (Mount Ortigara, June 1917). To both guage and harden the recruits' attitude to danger, on the sports field there was a peculiar contraption called the *dondolo* (or swing), consisting of two poles linked together by a bar, onto which a rope was tied: a large weight was attached to the end of the rope. The soldier was placed a set distance from the bar in relation to his height: the distance was calculated in such a way that as the weight swung round in an arc, it passed very near to the face of the recruit, hitting and knocking off his cap. Only a small number of the recruits did not flinch. For many, though, it was a matter of honour to succeed in this, and as a result many of them asked to retry until they had done so.

It is important to stress that these tests were not only used to screen the candidates, but were also a means of building up courage and confidence, in order to reach the so-called state of 'immunity to danger', which was the goal of all training exercises held at the school. Additionally, they were also a valuable means of improving the men's trust in their commanding officers and NCOs. Ten. Farina gave proof of this when he noted that due to the limited number of available soldiers, only five to ten per cent were rejected and returned to their previous units, so the other 95 per cent had to be trained anyway.

Following the somewhat severe opening episodes, the camp activities were directed towards specific military training. The school had several training areas, each of them dedicated to a different weapon or scenario: there were two areas for hand-grenade drill, three shooting ranges for sub-machine guns, machine guns and heavy guns, one firing range for flame-throwers, one area for tactical manoeuvres in front of obstacles, and most importantly, the 'dummy hill'.

'Green Flames' in training exercises with a Fiat 14 machine gun, summer 1918. This particular firing style permitted the rapid movement of the weapon from one fire position to another, although it was a little awkward for the gunner who had to carry it. The troops might be from XXIX Reparto, which was based in Val Lagarina at that time. (MGR 21/456)

The first training area for hand grenades allowed instructors to teach recruits the fundamentals of handling and throwing the Petardo Thevenot, the standard Arditi hand grenade. In fact, most recruits had never thrown such grenades, being used to the more common SIPE. In the second and more spacious hand-grenade area, the recruits received advanced training aimed at improving their efficiency against fixed and moving targets, while standing or running, from varying distances, alone, as part of a two-man team, or with the whole assault squad. After throwing the grenade, one Ardito was made to run ahead (to reduce the risk of being hit by the grenade's striker, the only lethal part of the Thevenot) and attack the enemy (represented on the training ground by a straw-filled dummy) with his dagger.

On the sub-machine gun range, which was also used for rifles and pistols, the Arditi *Pistolettieri* (sub-machine gunners) learned how to fire their weapons. They practised how to do so from the prone position, kneeling, standing, running, as well as drilling in how to reload quickly, how to maintain correct fire discipline and how to take cover in the field. On the machine-gun range, the weapon crews were taught how to shoot over the top of their own advancing troops (using fixed and moving devices as targets), how to organise barrage fire and how to change fire position quickly, following the assault. Similarly, the 65mm-gun crews were trained to provide supporting fire using mobile targets, as well as direct fire against pillboxes or machine-gun positions.

Part of the training process was devoted to enemy weapons, such as the Mannlicher rifle, the Schwarzlose machine guns, and the *stiehl* hand grenade. It was quite possible that, having exhausted his own ammunition or grenades, the Ardito would have to make use of the enemy's captured

Arditi flame-thrower operators during exercises in spring or summer 1918. The flame-thrower is the Italian twin-tank apparatus, first tested in December 1917 and used by the Arditi after May 1918. (Arch. Andrea Brambilla)

Ten. Ermes Rosa of XIII Reparto examines a captured Austro-Hungarian Schwarzlose machine gun. All Arditi were trained in using enemy weapons, in case their own ammunition ran out. (Coll. Dal Molin)

Arditi of the XXIX Reparto in training in Sabbionara D'Avio (in the Trentino sector) at the end of summer 1918. They are advancing under cover of smoke, probably made by mortar incendiary rounds, a tactic developed at Sdricca. (MGR 4/1453)

ones. The flame-thrower operators, after a training period at flame-thrower school in Montecchio Emilia (near Parma), practised firing against typical targets on the flame-thrower range.

A specific area for tactical training was built in order to represent all possible obstacles and dangerous situations, such as bunkers, machine-gun posts, pillboxes, and fire and communication trenches. Here the now competent Arditi candidates learnt the fundamental tactics necessary to storm or to flank an enemy position, how to act under incoming machine-gun fire, how to deal with a bunker in order to force the defenders to surrender, and how to pursue the retreating enemy. Some of these exercises were held with live counter-fire, in order to get the Arditi used to the sound of enemy weapons and to the feeling of being shot at.

Once the recruits had completed all the different levels of training, they were ready for full exercises, which consisted of real assaults, under live fire, on a perfect reproduction of an Austro-Hungarian fortified outpost, known in slang as the 'dummy hill' (*collina tipo*). These assaults were conducted by day or by night, under the beams of searchlights, and were repeated many times, in order to achieve perfect co-ordination between attacking troops, machine-gun covering fire and artillery support. Repeating the training day after day, and sometimes several times a day, also served to achieve 'immunity to danger'.

Contrary to rumours spread at the time, many sources play down the casualties taken during these extremely dangerous exercises. Ten. Farina stated that in more than 510 exercises held at Sdricca between 15 June and 24 October 1917, only one soldier died, several were lightly injured, and few seriously so. A different opinion was given by an anonymous lieutenant, the author of *The war memoirs of an Arditi officer*, who stated that 'on the training field, every day we saw wounded or dead men. It was easier to die at the Arditi School than in the trenches'. The truth as usual lies between the two extremes. One of the mottoes of the school was 'Sweat and blood today could save your life tomorrow', and being injured was considered a normal occurrence: it was also exploited as first-aid training for the two-man team.

Access to the training areas was carefully co-ordinated by training officers, so that different units or parts of them could rotate around them without wasting time, and so that all the facilities were in constant use and the soldiers could train continuously, without rest between different exercises. To ensure that the new recruits were kept on

The realistic nature of assault troop exercises is shown here: a wounded Ardito is carried on a stretcher by his fellow soldiers. In combat, stretchers were not used, it being the task of each Ardito to take care of his wounded 'partner'. (MGR 4/1464)

their toes, the *nonni* and NCOs would throw Thevenots into their tents or barracks: they were also woken up several times in the middle of the night to go on runs, to be ordered to get ready for action in full combat kit, or just to deprive them of sleep.

Ten.Col. Bassi not only prescribed military training, but also physical training. In the middle of the camp was an open field, which was used for ceremonies and sports. Running and gymnastics were prescribed every day: jumping over poles, ropes, walls, barbed-wire fences, trees, tables, hedgerows etc. prepared the men for the obstacles they would encounter on the battlefield. Magg. Freguglia, commander of the XXVII Reparto, noted proudly that more than 80 per cent of his soldiers were able to do a somersault.

The men also practised bayonet fighting, wrestling, and dagger combat in order to complement their specific military training. Swimming lessons were very much appreciated, and proved useful when a Reparto attacked the Austro-Hungarian trenches on the other side of the Piave River, thus earning the Arditi one of their many nicknames: the 'Piave Caymans'. After training, the use of the sports facilities was encouraged by officers who awarded prizes, and organised tournaments (football, wrestling, boxing, and running) in which the squads were pitted against each other, in order to improve the sense of belonging among the soldiers.

CLOTHING AND EQUIPMENT

Uniforms and insignia

According to Ten.Col. Bassi's instructions, the Ardito's uniform had to satisfy two criteria: firstly, it had to be comfortable and suitable for the assault soldier's needs, and secondly it had to be immediately recognisable, to identify the soldier as a member of a special unit. The uniform proposed by Bassi, which was not approved initially, was a mix of existing items, with a few key variations.

The tunic chosen was that of the Bersaglieri Ciclisti (mod.1910), which had shoulder straps, two breast pockets and a large hunting-style pocket on the back (useful for storing hand grenades), three large hidden

buttons and two buttoned belt loops: a key difference was a civilian-style open collar and reversed lapel. This tunic was the same for all Arditi regardless of rank, although photographs often show some officers wearing jackets with four pockets (two waist pockets were added), or tailor-made uniforms.

The collar patches (*mostrine*) featured double black flames, with the standard silver five-pointed star. The latter was in honour of one of Bassi's ancestors, Pietro F. Calvi: he was a hero of the Italian Risorgimento (Reunificiation) who was executed in 1855 by the Austrians, and who used to wear a black tie as a mark of association with the Carbonari. If the Assault unit was composed of Alpini or Bersaglieri, the flames were to be green or crimson respectively. Machine gunners wore the same flames as their comrades, but on blue rectangular backing.

A grey-green turtleneck woollen sweater, again used by Bersaglieri Ciclisti, was worn under the tunic: it had six small buttons running from the left shoulder to the neck. In warm weather, a grey-green shirt with a black tie was worn. In fact, especially after Caporetto, due to the lack of Ciclisti-style sweaters, most of the Arditi were issued the grey-green flannel shirt or, in exceptional cases, a white cotton shirt, both with a black tie, and a woollen, grey-green doublet.

Trousers were the light and comfortable knee-length Alpino (mod.1909) or Bersaglieri Ciclisti (mod.1910) models with two slanting pockets, a large waistband and an adjustable strap with a metal buckle on the back. The redundant grey-green woollen puttees were replaced by woollen socks, which were more comfortable, warmer and simpler to wear, although many Arditi continued to wear puttees. The Ardito usually wore Alpino-style hobnail boots (mod.1912), although the original intent, which was never realised, was to select new boots that were heavier than the normal full dress shoes and lighter than the combat boots.

Initially, the headgear for soldiers was the standard mod.1915 felt képi (nicknamed the *scodellino* or 'dish') or the mod.1907 hat: after Caporetto, the standard soldier's headgear became the black felt fez, derived from the Bersaglieri's red and blue one. NCOs and officers bore the normal hat reserved for their rank (the mod.1907). The 'Green Flames' kept the Alpino-style felt hat, with crow (soldiers) and eagle (officers) feathers, while usually exchanging the standard insignia for the Ardito's badge. It is not clear if 'Crimson Flames' adopted the black fez or kept their bicolour one (evidence for both cases exists).

BELOW On the left is the Esploratori badge, in black woollen yarn (this was in silver for NCOs and in gold for officers). On the right is the 'VE' valour badge, with its award document in the middle. The 'VE' came in hand-sewn silver yarn, or was machine-sewn in black woollen yarn for reasons of camouflage. (Coll. Andrea Brambilla)

R. ESERCITO ITALIANO
ni
(2) 2ª *Battagl.* (3) 8ª *Compagnia*

CONCESSIONE DEL DISTINTIVO
PER MILITARI ARDITI

Il *Sold. Scotti Paolo* (4)

per aver dato ripetute prove di arditezza
è autorizzato a fregiarsi del distintivo pre-
detto.

Il Comandante del *Reggimento*

There were two different models of cap badge. The first, although quite rare, represented a burning grenade with a *gladium* inside, encircled by laurel and oak leaves, with the flames pointing to the right. The second, 'standard' model consisted of two crossed *gladia* on a burning grenade with flames pointing to the left, and the number of the Reparto written in Roman numerals. After the foundation of the Assault Divisions, the number had to be written in Arabic numerals on the cap badge, and in Roman numerals on the shoulder straps. Both badges were sewn in black wool. It is not rare, however, to find the sleeve badge sewn on the headgear or on the helmet cover. No badge was allowed on the fez.

The sleeve badge was quite distinctive and the symbol that Ten.Col. Bassi had intended: a Roman *gladium* (symbolising honour and courage), with the eagle-headed handle (symbolising power), was encircled by laurel (symbolising victory) and oak (symbolising loyalty and force) leaves, with the Savoy knot binding the weapon to the stems. Another reference to the Royal family was the Savoy motto 'FERT' (of unknown origin) on the crossbar. The badge, to be worn on the left sleeve, was hand-sewn on grey-green cloth, with gold yarn for officers, silver yarn for NCOs and black yarn for troopers. A machine-sewn badge on grey cotton cloth was also produced for soldiers. The badge was such an identifying feature that the auxiliary troops of the Assault Army Corps were not entitled to wear it, although they wore the black flames on the normal infantry uniform. However, in order to foster and denote a sense of belonging, the Bersaglieri assigned to the Assault Divisions were given the assault badge, but denied the right to wear the open collar uniform.

The relaxed attitudes among the Arditi with regard to compliance was such that it is difficult to find the same uniform worn in any photographed group. Indeed, each Ardito tried, and was allowed, to add a personal touch to his uniform, by adopting a captured belt or dagger, by retaining the cap badge of his former unit, sewing the badge on the opposite sleeve if the right one was already occupied, subtley varying his clothing so as not to have the same appearance as his comrades. The officers, called upon to enforce the regulations, were the first to make personal changes.

Equipment

The principal characteristic of the early Ardito's equipment was its lightness and simplicity, using only what was necessary to bring victory in his assault. For this reason, the equipment was reduced to the mod.16 steel helmet, a leather belt holding two twin cartridge pouches, an entrenching tool, a haversack for hand grenades, a canteen and a gas mask, saving around 4.5kg of weight compared to standard infantry gear. When the Assault Army Corps was formed, in reflection of the newer and wider range of deployment options, each Ardito was ordered to carry a haversack containing rations for two days, a mess tin, a spoon, a metal cup, a first-aid kit, a spare pair of socks and underwear, a handkerchief, the fez, a sandbag, a tent section, and a blanket.

The helmet, a two-piece Italian version of the French Adrian, was certainly the worst helmet to be used in the whole war, being more fragile than the original model, and with a thickness of only 0.7mm it was practically useless. On the other hand, it weighed only 700/800g, compared to the 1,300/1,400g of the enemy helmets. The helmets were stencilled with the Arditi's badge or with the number of the units in Roman numerals (or both in exceptional cases). When worn with the cover (sometimes made out of sandbags) for camouflage purposes, it was normal to sew on the sleeve badge, usually the machine-sewn one. The 'Crimson Flames' also added the Bersaglieri's famous cockerel feather plume.

The two twin pouches, sometimes reduced to one, were of grey-green dyed leather, and each of them held 48 rounds. Because there were two belt loops already sewn onto the tunic, the standard double chest belt was eliminated.

The haversack mod.1907/09 was made of grey waterproof cotton fabric, while its leather parts were grey-green. It could be worn alone as a single sack, or fastened to the rear of the larger pack (although this was impossible for an Ardito to do). The mod.1917 aluminum canteen was often attached to the haversack: it was covered in grey-green cloth, and was intended to replace the old mod.1907 wooden water bottle (in production since 1851), although the latter continued in service until much later.

The Ardito kept his entrenching tool in a leather carrier attached to his belt: this could be a shovel, a pickaxe (the most common), or a mattock. It is reported that on some occasions the entrenching tools were used as trench weapons, when the dagger was lost, in close-quarter fighting. Some Ardito also carried wire-cutters, although the larger wire-cutters were carried by the engineer troops of the specialist platoon (in the early period).

An essential item of equipment was the gas mask, despite the fact that there is no evidence that the Arditi were ever attacked by gas. Until Caporetto, where it proved itself to be useless, the whole Italian Army was equipped with the *maschera antigas Polivalente*. It was made of 32 or 64 cotton filters and was carried in its grey-green tin, wood or cardboard box. Following its poor performance in battle, the more effective and more practical British-made SBR (Small Box Respirator) mask was delivered to the Italian Army and became the standard mask. It was carried on the chest in its khaki bag, which contained the filter box that was linked to the mask by a rubberised tube.

It is important to stress that the equipment was not considered invariable. At the discretion of the commanding officer, depending on the particular action or on terrain or weather, many of the tools could be left behind. Only with the development of the Assault Army Corps was the Ardito's haversack considered to be an essential item, because it granted two to four days' worth of logistical autonomy. Nevertheless, when necessary, the haversack was left at the starting position, to be recovered after the action.

WEAPONS

Individual weapons

Each Ardito was equipped with a *Moschetto mod.'91 da cavalleria* (cavalry carbine mod.1891) or a *Moschetto '91 TS* ('TS' stands for *Truppe Speciali*, 'Special Troops'). Both were derived from the standard Italian Mannlicher-Carcano mod.1891 bolt-action rifle, generally known as 'the 91'. However, they were shorter (920mm vs. 1,280mm) and lighter (3.1kg vs. 3.8kg, or 4.1kg with bayonet), while maintaining the same ballistic and mechanical characteristics.

There was a preference for the cavalry carbine, which had a 38cm fixed, triangular, folding bayonet, in order to save weight and provide a more flexibile bayonet, while the TS had a standard mod.'91 bayonet,

A sergeant in combat uniform, with the characteristic cockerel-feather plume on the helmet, and crimson-flame collar patches. He is armed with a cavalry '91 carbine and with a file-handle dagger, and carries the two twin cartridge pouches. (MGR 90/81)

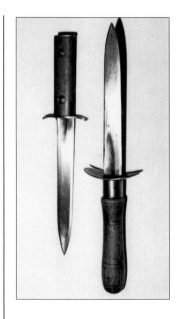

Two standard-issue daggers, both derived from the Vetterly bayonet. The one on the left is the most common form, while the other is known as the 'file-handle' version. (Courtesy MNA Torino, photo Federico Cavallero)

but featured a different fixing point. Auxiliary troops of the Reparti were issued the standard mod.'91 rifle. Although of smaller calibre (6.5mm – 6.5 × 52) than enemy rifles, namely the Steyr-Mannlicher mod.1895 cal. 8mm and the Mauser M98 cal. 7.92mm, and consequently less powerful, the Italian rifle had two advantages: it had one more round in the magazine (six in all) and (with particular regard to the Austro-Hungarian rifle) it featured a symmetrical magazine that could be loaded upside down. The latter was a much-appreciated point at night or in the midst of an action.

Machine gunners, sub-machine gunners, flame-thrower operators and NCOs all carried the heavy six-round Bodeo mod.1889 cal.10.35 revolver, with folding trigger (mod.A). The holster for this was worn on the right-hand side, and had a lanyard around the neck. Officers were armed with the mod.B Bodeo with trigger guard, or else an automatic pistol such as the Glisenti mod.1910, or its imitator the Brixia mod.1912 cal. 9mm (9 × 19), which featured a seven-round magazine, or the newly designed Beretta mod.15, also with a seven-round 9mm Glisenti magazine (an eight-round 7.65mm version also existed). The latter was the forefather of the modern Beretta M9 (Italian mod.92), now adopted by the US armed forces.

Each member of the assault units, irrespective of rank, carried a dagger. This distinctive weapon was well suited to the Arditi's style of combat: it was more ergonomic than a standard bayonet, being lighter in weight and with a grip on the handle, and of course it was perfect as a silent weapon of surprise. It was a common myth among the Austro-Hungarian troops that the Arditi were experts with daggers, and that they all came from Sicily, a place famous for its duels and swordsmanship. The standard-issue assault dagger was manufactured by shortening the bayonet of the old Italian Vetterli-Vitali mod.1870 rifle. Using the same blade, many different handle styles were fashioned, the daggers being known as file handles. Other daggers came from field modifications to the standard bayonet mod.'91 or to captured Steyr-Mannlicher bayonets, one of the most sought-after models being the chromed dagger issued to NCOs. In many cases soldiers proudly displayed captured Austro-Hungarian assault daggers, called *sturmmesser*, particularly postwar during the Fiume incident and in the early Fascist paramilitary units. Daggers were also commonly worn off duty.

The other distinctive weapon of the Ardito was the hand grenade. The standard grenades were the *Petardo Offensivo mod. Thevenot* (Thevenot) and the *Petardo Offensivo sistema Olergon* (P.O.): both had a limited range, but were powerful. The splinters from these were actually relatively

A collection of handguns used by the Arditi: on the top left, a Bodeo mod.1889A for troopers and NCOs with folding trigger, and below this an mod.1889B for officers, with trigger guard: both are 10.35mm calibre. On the upper right is the Glisenti 9mm calibre pistol, while below this is the Beretta mod.1915 9mm calibre gun. (Courtesy MNA Torino, photo Federico Cavallero)

harmless, the dangerous part being the striker, but the noise and the blast were impressive.

The Thevenot, of French design, was manufactured in France and in Italy: the Italian version had a red star on the body, the French one a red circle. It was a metal cylinder, with a hole in the main body, where the safety pin kept the detonator away from the charge. When thrown, the removal of the safety pin freed the striker, and the impact on the target detonated the explosive. It weighed around 400g with 160g of Echo explosive, while its range was only 5–10 metres. The P.O. consisted of a tin container filled with 150g of Echo or TNT, with an Olergon fuse head screwed on top: its total weight was

The '*Petardo Thevenot*', the preferred hand grenade of the Arditi. The fabric strap kept the safety mechanism in place, and the grenade was primed only when thrown. Its effective range was less than 10m, and the resultant splinters were rarely lethal. (MGR)

400g. After pulling the safety ring and throwing the grenade, its detonation was caused by percussion. It had a range of 10–15 metres. Both hand grenades were available in an incendiary version, respectively the *Petardo Incendiario Thevenot* and the *Petardo Incendiario sistema Olergon* (P.I.), both with the same characteristics. They were used to create smoke curtains during attacks or to clear bunkers and dugouts. Although post-war and propaganda iconography often represented the Ardito with the classical SIPE (*Società Italiana Prodotti Esplosivi*) grenade in hand, this type of defensive grenade was not used, primarily due to its weight (550g) and effective range of over 20m (limited range was important to the Arditi).

Initially, when Reparti d'Assalto were employed for limited operations, each Ardito was normally given 12 Thevenots and 72 rifle cartridges, given the relative ease of receiving spare ammunition and grenades. Certain soldiers, usually signal troops, were equipped with two sandbags full of Thevenots, and were tasked with resupplying their comrades.

Assault Army Corps instructions fixed the standard issue at 120 rifle rounds and only six hand grenades: these were based on lessons learned, when some operations failed because units ran out of ammunition before being relieved. It is reasonable to assume that the first assault waves were given additional hand grenades. It is also important to stress that the Assault Army Corps had a logistical system that the normal Reparto did not, so resupply of the units was quicker and more efficient.

Crew-served weapons

The 1917 Reparto d'Assalto had 24 sub-machine guns (two per platoon, eight per company) and eight machine guns (two per company, plus two attached to the HQ of the Reparto). The 3rd Company also had a section with two 65mm guns. The 4th Company, which acted as the replacement and training unit for the others, had a section of 15 flame-throwers.

The *Pistola Mitragliatrice FIAT mod.15* 9mm sub-machine gun, also known as the *Officine Villar Perosa (OVP) – Revelli mod.1915* (or, more simply, 'Villar Perosa') was the standard Italian sub-machine gun of World War I and the first sub-machine gun ever adopted. With its high rate of fire (25 rounds per second), its 54cm length, and weighing in at only 6.5kg, it was perfect for the Arditi's needs. In fact Ten.Col. Bassi personally designed a carrying system and a bipod, discarding the heavy shield (26kg). The Villar Perosa had twin parallel barrels, linked at the rear by the loading/firing mechanism and in the centre by a circular plate: they were fed by two magazines, each containing 25 rounds of 9mm Glisenti ammunition. A skilled gunner could draw three different bursts from each magazine, but a major drawback of this weapon was the manner in which it wasted ammunition. Four soldiers manned the gun, and three of these had to carry two haversacks filled with 30 spare magazines each. Including the magazines carried by the gunner himself, each Villar Perosa had around 5,000 rounds available.

The standard machine gun of the Italian Army was the 6.5mm *FIAT-Revelli mod.1914*, also known as the Fiat 14. It was produced in two different models, both water-cooled, one with a smooth cooling jacket, and the other with a corrugated jacket for improved heat dispersal. The gun was fed by a 50-round box magazine: it had a theoretical firing rate of 500 rounds per minute, but in reality fired no more than 200, due to the need to change magazines. The 50 cartridges were in 10 compartments, each of five rounds, with each column featuring an elevation spring. As the machine gun fired the five rounds, the magazine advanced by one column. The gun weighed 38.5kg and consisted of two parts, the gun (17kg) and the tripod (21.5kg). Each machine-gun squad was manned by one gunner, four assistants and three ammunition carriers, and was issued only 20,000 rounds, 6,000 immediately available, with the remaining 14,000 brought by mules.

One of the tactical innovations of the Arditi was the close co-operation between artillery, machine guns and assault troops, so each Reparto received a mule-carried section of two 65/17 mountain guns, which were more mobile than similar weapons (in particular the old

The Fiat mod.15, known as the *Villar Perosa*, was the first sub-machine gun ever adopted by an army. Normally, it carried two 25-round 9mm-cal. magazines, but only one is shown here. The bipod was invented by Ten.Col. Bassi and allowed the weapon to be deployed in all situations. (Courtesy MNA Torino, photo Federico Cavallero)

Arditi Corporal (Caporal Maggiore)

B

A 'Death Company' attack, the Carso plains, October 1915

Arditi training school, Sdricca di Manzano, 1917

C

Captain (Capitano), XXIX Reparto

D

Assault on the Col Moschin, 16 June 1918

E

F

Preparing for the flame-thrower attack on Mt. San Gabriele, 4 September 1917

First aid on the banks of the Piave River, end of October 1918

G

FIUME O MORTE

2

ARDISCO NON ORDISCO

1

A VALORE MILITARE

3

HIC · MANE BIMVS · OPTIME

4

Gabriele D'Annunzio in Fiume, late 1919

H

Bettica) in use at the time. Weighing 460kg, and broken down into four parts, it was an artillery piece much appreciated for its accuracy and ease of operation. It had an effective range of 6,500 metres and used two different types of ammunition: a steel round weighing 4.27kg (250g of Trotyl) and a shrapnel round, with 216 steel grains (each weighing 11g), for a total of 4.079kg.

The flame-throwers were used for the first time in September 1917, but were soon considered ill suited for assault work as a result of their slow operation. The initial section was disbanded, and they were not added to other units. After the re-organisation of May 1918, each Reparto was again given three flame-thrower sections, for a total of 18 weapons.

The portable flame-throwers in use in 1917 were probably the imported French *Schilt n.3 bis* model or the modified Italian version, the *Schilt n.3 bis OFC*. Both had a 15-litre fuel tank, with a smaller tank (1.4 litre) for compressed air: a burning wad ignited the fuel spray. Due to their bulky weight (22kg empty), they were soon substituted with the Italian-designed DLF (*Direzione Lanciafiamme*, or Flame-thrower Department), which was similar to the original but was lighter (18/20kg when the 12-litre tank was half full) and easier to operate. In December 1917 another Italian flame-thrower was made available, with the clumsy name of *Apparato tipo italiano a due serbatoi accoppiati* (Italian Twin Tank Apparatus). A small CO_2 cylinder operated the two twin fuel tanks, each with a capacity of 6 litres, and the fuel burned by passing through an automatic igniter. The fuel for all types was composed of five parts of tar oil and one part

Two seamen of the Reggimento Marina (Navy Regiment). The soldier on the left could be a regimental Ardito, given his dagger, his Moschetto TS gun, and the way he has fastened his tunic. Both soldiers are equipped with the British SBR gas mask in its khaki sack. (MGR 90/82)

of oil, or carbon disulphide. Flame-thrower sections were also equipped with special asbestos masks and gloves, much-hated items that were never widely employed.

With the birth of the Assault Army Corps, in June 1918, each Reparto was given a section of four Stokes mortars, which were used instead of the two 65mm guns to destroy obstacles and defensive strongpoints. In the Assault Army Corps the 65mm guns were maintained and were concentrated in a Mountain Artillery Group (consisting of three batteries) for each Assault Division. The distribution of automatic weapons was changed: the machine guns were concentrated in one machine-gun company, while two autonomous sub-machine-gun sections were instituted for every company (each with six weapons), rather than keeping the Villar Perosa in the assault platoons.

The Stokes 76mm (3in.) mortar, built in Italy under British licence, had a range of about 800m and fired several types of shell: explosive, smoke, incendiary, with British (timed) or Italian (percussive) fuse heads. A squad of five soldiers was sufficient to man the 40kg weapon, which could be disassembled into three parts (the barrel, the bipod and a 20kg base plate). The Italian version differed from the British one in that it had a folding bipod and an exposed elevating screw. A later Italian version was of 81mm calibre.

To increase obstacle destruction capabilities, each Assault Division also had a section of four 37mm (37/12) guns, called '37Fs'. Manned by three men, each gun had a range of 600–1,500 metres and fired a light steel shell (640g, with 65g of explosive); due to the small calibre, a shrapnel shell was not produced. Being mounted on wheels and weighing only 56kg, it was more mobile than the mortar, and although it had to operate in the open, it was perfect for firing on trenches, machine-gun dugouts and pillboxes.

DAILY LIFE

Most of the information we have concerning Ardito daily life relates to time spent at the training school at Sdricca, but we can be sure that, at least until the institution of the Assault Army Corps, the daily routine outside of combat followed the same pattern.

The wake-up call was given at 0600 hours by a couple of trench mortar rounds, just in case anyone had forgotten the reason why he was there. After bathing in the Natisone River, training began and lasted until 1800 hours, with pauses for food. Free time followed half an hour's moral instruction, given by an officer or a chaplain. During summer

months training was halted between 1000 and 1500 hours, and in autumn it ended at dusk. Some would spend their time at the sports facilities (boxing tournaments were very common), others would rest in their barracks or tents, while others still might leave camp to visit the small town of Manzano. Taps was supposedly at 2200 hours, but the duty officer would rarely check that all soldiers were in. In contrast though, it was absolutely unthinkable to miss First Call the next morning.

During this quiet period, a certain amount of contact with local civilians occurred. Even though the townspeople were broadly happy to play host to the young Arditi, or at least, their officers, it is also true that sometimes (perhaps quite often) their animals fell victim to the endless appetite of the troops. In fact, one of the common nicknames given to the Arditi was 'the hen-stealers'. Another way of procuring additional food was by fishing in the Natisone River, obviously in typical Ardito fashion: the missing boxes of Thevenot grenades were compensated for by the smell of fresh fish being cooked by mess assistants. The preferred method of finding food though was the so-called 'supply assault', which usually took place before an operation so that it would be forgotten in the course of the action.

Father Reginaldo Giuliani, the most famous chaplain of the Arditi. Renowned for his outstanding courage (he earned one silver and two Bronze Valour Medals in World War I, and a posthumous Gold Valour Medal in the Abyssinian conflict), he was tireless in giving advice and guidance, looking after his soldiers' spiritual needs, helping them physically, and inspiring them before and after battle – and often during it too. These were typical duties for chaplains, who were identified by a red cross on their chest, as shown here. This is one of the few photos that shows the first-style cap badge of the Arditi. (Arch. Ufficio Storico FNAI)

Sometimes a pair of lorries 'lost' their way to the camp and 'by chance' arrived in front of a supply depot. A quick attack with Thevenot grenades usually convinced the frightened depot guards to surrender. Cartons of cigarettes, wine and rations would find their way into the Arditi's camp, often with the complicity of NCOs and officers. Beyond the daily ration allowed, alcohol was strictly forbidden in camp and was not sold in the canteen. However, questions were rarely asked if a soldier came back a little drunk, as long as his condition did not interfere with training.

Another area where there was considerable personal freedom (and consequently numerous complaints from civilians) was with local women. The myth of the Ardito as a bold andfearless soldier made some of the troops both more attractive and more determined. The complaints even reached the Supreme Command, which called for an immediate restoration of discipline and for the placement of the camps to be moved to open country, far from towns.

Often, the local sections of Carabinieri (the Italian Military Police) were issued orders not to bother with drunk or unruly Arditi. This branch of the Army was probably the most hated of all by the regular soldiers, principally because they manned the firing squads and maintained discipline behind the front line, with powers to shoot those suspected of cowardice or mutiny on sight. On many occasions the Carabinieri were victims of pranks or even assaults by the Arditi, sometimes resulting in legal issues. A famous trial was held in which three Arditi were accused of having ambushed (with hand grenades, no less) a patrol of Carabinieri that was returning some 'Black Flames' to Sdricca to be imprisoned. Some of the policemen were seriously injured, and a court martial followed. The Arditi, who risked the death sentence, were sentenced to 20 years in prison, to be served after the war (should they survive, of course).

The relationships with other units were also problematic, due to the Arditi's bravado and the regular infantry's resentment of their privileges. In truth, they rarely came across each other, notably because assault troops were not attached to a particular regiment or division but were supplementary troops of the Army Corps. This also intensified their alienation. The Arditi did not enjoy a good reputation. Ten. Giudici wrote of the 1st Army's officers:

They had never seen Arditi before, they did not know what assault troops were for, they ignored our life, our tactics, our way of being, and thought in good faith that we were jailbirds, the dregs of society, butchers and at the same time animals for the slaughter, beasts and members of punishment brigades. They changed their mind after a while.

A rare image of Arditi of the Italian Royal Navy, taken during a ceremony in late-1918 in Milan. In World War I, the Italian Navy formed a 'Navy Regiment', which included regimental Arditi. (Arch. Ufficio Storico FNAI)

It is interesting to note too that the Commission on Caporetto labelled the Arditi as a 'gang of bandits', 'praetorians', and 'unscrupulous people'. Some Reparti did demonstrate ill discipline in the aftermath of their re-organisation following Caporetto, though this was by no means extraordinary. In fact, the chain of command was not rigid and was often quite different to that of regular infantry units. Punishment was also different, with the emphasis on increased training for offenders rather than courts martial and jail sentences. Many memoirs state that corporal punishment was sometimes adopted for more serious offences, but the maximum penalty was considered the return to one's former unit.

When Magg. Messe and Magg. Freguglia arrived at their Reparti in February 1918, respectively the VI (later IX) and V (later XXVII), they found disorder and a veritable lack of control. Only after dismissing the worst elements and transferring some of the less-determined officers, while intensifying training, was order restored, allowing the units to regain their combat readiness. Discipline would certainly have been quite different to the normal standards of the Italian Army, given that when the Army Corps was instituted the commander Ten.Gen. Francesco Saverio Grazioli called for tighter rules, and for an immediate return to the customary standards of discipline. It was part of the 'normalisation' process, which stemmed from Grazioli's vision of the

The XXIX Reparto found time to build a monumental gate at the entrance to their camp at Vo' Sinistro (Trentino). Here they are shown receiving their battle flag in summer 1918. Being 'Green Flames', their standard is adorned with an eagle. (MGR 4/1371)

assault troops under his command as being part of a larger organisation that looked beyond the traditions and status of the individual Reparto.

Things changed though when the Arditi received the order to go into action. Many memoirs recall how the order to leave camp was welcomed by shouts of joy, and the columns of lorries, mainly the Fiat BL 18 or Fiat 15 Ter, would trail noise and smoke behind them, caused by war songs (often graphic) and by shots fired into the air or exploding hand grenades. Ten. Giudici wrote:

> We went into battle as any army would, because war was a joy to us, the fulfilment of our dreams, the object of our passion. We went into battle as Arabs and Askari do, as any other people born and raised for war do, screaming with joy, singing ourselves hoarse, bugling and shooting, exciting and stirring the people along the road.

Mario Carli, the founder of the Arditi Association, left this testimony:

> Every time the 2nd Army's Arditi went into action it was not with a sense of resignation and duty, nor with the forced smile of self-control, but with outbursts of barbaric joy … they left in lorries in showers of dust, saying goodbye to comrades with exultations, swearing on their daggers that they would win.

THE ARDITO IN BATTLE

Tactics

The Arditi's operational doctrine featured numerous innovations, adding to those already made to the uniforms, equipment and weapons, which were based on combat experiences of the officers, particularly Ten.Col. Bassi.

Experience had taught that most regular-infantry attacks failed due to the long delay between the end of preparatory shelling and the arrival of the infantry, thus allowing the defenders precious time to come out of their shelters and prepare for the asssualt. Bassi's innovative idea involved co-ordination between artillery, machine guns and the infantry assault, in order to exploit the particular characteristics of each of them to the full. Artillery fire became an accompanying process as opposed to a preparatory phase. The troops thus had to advance under an arc of artillery and machine-gun fire, in order to be as close as possible to the enemy position at the end of the shelling, from where they would rush ahead throwing dozens of hand grenades, to keep the defenders in their shelters.

Things did not always go according to plan. On Mt. San Gabriele, on 4 September 1917, after 20 minutes of shelling, the Arditi attack began under the arc of fire: however, many Arditi were killed by Italian shells, because they ran too quickly towards the enemy. Ten. Giudici reported:

A vivid image of the attack executed by Arditi on Mt. Fratta beyond the Isonzo River on 18 August 1918. It was the first combat employment of assault troops. Here they are shown emerging from the smoke caused by incendiary shells. (MGR 1/116)

At dawn, all the Arditi were standing in the trenches, waiting for orders. The calm was impressive. Not even a shot. At 5.30, without any warning, we heard a sound like the roaring of a sudden storm. ... Our guns pounded the mountain, and shattered, savaged and broke up the landscape ... An order was passed throughout the line. 'Ready ... Forward!' And the trench tops were soon passed by; the assault began very quickly, colouring the hillside grey-green, mounted the rocks, shadowed in the woods, straight towards the enemy's trenches. The first Arditi fell, hit by our artillery, impatient to reach the enemy ... Then, shortly after, all the guns stopped, and a sepulcral silence reigned. Then a colossal scream, heard throughout the front. And the true, terrible fighting began.

In order not to give the defenders time to organise a new line of resistance, attacks had to be executed using two different types of squads. The assault squads, armed with daggers and hand grenades, were tasked with eliminating the enemy lookouts, passing through (or over) the first line of defence and targeting the heart of the enemy defensive system, such as bunkers or command shelters. The attack squads were armed with carbines, daggers and hand grenades, and were to destroy any remaining pockets of resistance, clear the trenches and to prepare the captured zone to be defended against an enemy counter-attack, while awaiting the arrival of a wave of regular infantrymen. Sub-machine-gun squads gave close cover, in order to provide immediate automatic-weapons support where it was needed, while direct fire from 65mm (later also 37mm) guns was aimed at pillboxes or dugouts. When available, flame-throwers were used as a short-range clearing tool.

On Mt. San Gabriele, after the conquest of the first line, the Arditi had to destroy several fortified outposts and clear the system of bunkers and underground passages from which a continuous stream of defenders sortied. The same Ten. Giudici recalled:

Arditi on a Fiat BL 18 lorry in Bassano del Grappa just prior to leaving for action on Mt. Grappa, in spring 1918. Different styles of uniform and articles of clothing can be seen, including flannel shirts, black ties, woollen sweaters, puttees, woollen socks, and three different types of headgear (the Alpino hat, worn by the flag-bearer, the 'scodellino' worn by the man to his left, and the berretto mod.1907, worn by the other Arditi). (Coll. Dal Molin)

It was a fierce struggle. All the trench defenders were slaughtered … The battle fragmented into a hundred smaller ones, and broke out around the rocks, in the midst of barbed-wire entanglements, in the bunkers and in the tunnels … The passages had been blocked with Thevenots, the entrances torched with flame-throwers … The bowels of the mountain were full of the enemy … We fought in the dark, in a never-ending labyrinth, with hand grenades, dagger thrusts, shovel hits, punches, kicks and bites. At ten o'clock, we were masters of the field.

The keys to a successful attack were, in the words of Ten. Farina, good preparation, manoeuvrability, a rapid strike, and the element of surprise. In fact, rather than using the standard company or battalion frontal advance in line, a suicidal tactic against a fortified trench with automatic weapons, the Arditi developed a more flexible and rewarding tactic: a manoeuvering attack made by several perfectly trained squads, that were able to exploit all topographical advantages and could understand where the priority lay during an operation. These skills were enhanced by a detailed study of the situation, achieved by inspections of the line by the officers of the Reparto, the support of aerial photographic reconnaissance and intelligence briefings and, when time permitted, the construction of a model of the zone to be attacked at the training camp. The attack orders were very detailed, containing information about the topographical and tactical situation, giving instructions to supporting artillery, probable enemy reactions, the assigned tasks for each unit and clearly defined primary and secondary targets, in order to give officers all the information needed to achieve their goal and exploit the hoped-for success.

When the co-ordination and preparatory work did not succeed, great problems were faced by the Arditi, as vividly reported by Ten. Businelli regarding the assault on Mt. Asolone, on 24 June 1918:

> We are in front of new barbed-wire fences and, moreover, exposed to a hellish machine-gun fire … In addition, enemy artillery shells the crest, hitting friend and foe, trying to keep the position. Our losses are impressive; the stubborn entanglements do not allow any movement forward, and the merciless Schwarzlosen blast volleys and volleys of shot, and the defenders ceaselessly throw dozens of hand grenades. Our artillery did not cause any damage to the well-fortified enemy trenches, and our impotent waves are breaking on the granite defences.

The Arditi did manage to take the mountain, partly thanks to the heroic example of their standard-bearer, who led the survivors in their charge over the enemy defence.

At the heart of Bassi's new tactical approach was the introduction of the two-man team, a true revolution in military and psychological terms. In order to form a single tactical element, two Arditi were supposed to live together at all times, whether in training or off duty. Each one had to take care of the other, providing first aid or evacuation if the other was wounded, and he was authorised to leave him only on his partner's death. This spirit of emulation and the close relationship between the

Trenches on Mt. Fratta during the first combat deployment of the Reparti d'Assalto on 18 August 1918. Smoke covers the movement of the Arditi in no-man's land. (MGR 1/114)

two soldiers was an effective force strengthener, and introduced a radical concept into soldiering: individual responsibility. Soldiers were able to take decisions without orders; they lost all sense of hesitation and lost several bad habits (such as the risk-filled tendency to regroup in dangerous situations and await orders), thus allowing them to conduct flexible and selective assaults.

The experience of battle

When close to the enemy, the Arditi were the masters of the forceful, decisive and rapid strike. In addition, the Ardito's training and mental preparation pushed him to prolong his effort, searching for another target to attack or pursuing the rattled enemy, rather than stopping to rest. Ten. Businelli reported the following of IX Reparto's assault on Mt. Fenilon on 15 June 1918:

> We approach the enemy line, as shells land like drumbeats. Suddenly, we yell a formidable '*A noi!*' The artillery stops at once and hundreds of Thevenots, after one or two seconds, fall on the enemy trenches. There is a tremendous blast, soon followed by machine-gun bursts. Some Arditi fall, but the others pass over the barbed wire and spread out on the mountain top, searching out the enemy in every recess, in every trench, in every bunker, shouting '*Messe! A Noi!*' They are like devils, passing from one target to another: a Thevenot, a jet of flame-thrower, and away! To the next one! … After a while everything is broken up, destroyed. The Austrian soldiers see the Arditi ahead, on the left, on the right, behind them … We stop only when we do not find any more of the enemy.

To achieve the essential factor of surprise, a difficult feat to achieve in trench warfare, the Arditi developed the above-quoted style of advance during shelling, with the lengthening of fire at the last minute, while protracted shelling took place in the adjacent sectors as a diversion. Sometimes Arditi preferred to attack without any artillery support, using mortar shells to blow up the barbed-wire fences: these were detonated by the engineer troops of the specialist platoon. The fact that assault troops arrived directly from the rear to perform the assault often meant the enemy was unaware that the Arditi were organising an attack, unlike normal offensive operations where the organisation took several days and involved large movements of troops. Italian intelligence reports stated that the enemy troops were astonished by the appearance of hundreds of pairs of Arditi (who were extremely mobile and difficult to aim at) rushing against the enemy with a dagger clenched between their teeth and hand grenades in both hands, in a deluge of shells, bullets and hand grenades.

When the enemy understood they were faced with the Arditi, their hands were raised more readily in surrender. In some cases many Austro-Hungarians did not understand what was going on and found themselves taken prisoner. A small escort of some lightly wounded Arditi was usually adequate for guiding the prisoners back to the Italian lines, and on some occasions merely pointing them towards the Italian trenches was sufficient.

In at least one case, however, it was reported that the Arditi took revenge on a certain artillery battery that had been shelling Bassano del Grappa, and killed all the prisoners taken. The protesting Austrian commanding officer was told by the Italian commander 'It's your business!' Often the Arditi were given the order not to take prisoners, in order to let the advance continue. It was a common belief that the same treatment would befall them should they be taken prisoner, and that it was better not to be capured alive. However, we know that the Arditi did take large numbers of prisoners, and so we can assume that such behaviour was not common.

Combat organisation

The Reparto d'Assalto organised by Ten.Col. Bassi was completely autonomous, except for the supporting fire, and possessed all necessary weapons and equipment to achieve its goals. The unit had three assault companies totalling about 700 men, with four assault platoons of riflemen and one of specialist troops (machine gunners, engineers, signal troops); each platoon had four squads (one assault and three attack) with five two-man teams each; sub-machine guns and machine guns were assigned to the platoons, while the 3rd company also had a section of two 65mm guns. The 4th company, which in the I Reparto had a flame-thrower section, served as a replacement and training unit (see Table 5.1 on page 53).

With respect to a regular infantry battalion, which had about 1,000 men, the Reparto d'Assalto had an overwhelming superiority in automatic weapons (two machine guns and 20 more sub-machine guns), and even possessed its own mobile (though somewhat limited) artillery.

The replacement system was innovative: instead of providing replacements on a soldier-by-soldier basis, the whole unit (a squad, a platoon or the whole company) was changed, in order not to destroy the bonds between the soldiers and with their officers. The replaced unit would then begin training new recruits, taking the place of the previous one in the replacement company. The same system was maintained within the Reparti d'Assalto di Marcia as well, and allowed a continuously high rate of availability of the units, and guaranteed a trained reserve, able to fight if necessary.

With the reorganisation of 1918, the company remained the basic unit, but lost its specialist platoon (machine guns were concentrated in

One of the most famous photos of the Arditi: soldiers of XII Reparto celebrate the end of an engagement in the Lower Piave sector in June 1918. The raised dagger and the war cry 'A noi!' ('To us!') formed the Ardito way of presenting arms. This motif was developed specifically for the Arditi by Magg. Freguglia of XXVII Reparto. (MGR 3/1236)

Another famous photograph: Arditi with Stokes mortars after the June 1918 actions on the Piave River. The soldier on the lower left holds a Moschetto TS carbine: the bicycle to the right is the one issued to Bersaglieri Ciclisti. (MGR 3/1235)

a separate company) and the sub-machine guns were concentrated into two autonomous sections for each company. The total number of men was about 900, with the number of sub-machine guns increased to 36. The replacement company was eliminated, because each Army and each Assault Division had its own replacement unit. The Reparto lost its 65mm guns, while gaining a mortar section and three flame-thrower sections, plus a supply section (see Table 5.2).

It was a tactical burden little appreciated by the officers of the Sdricca school, but it was a step in the direction of assimilating the Arditi into the infantry units, denying them their exclusive status and giving the whole Army the same training Arditi had. With regard to this, it is important to note that, in the replacement unit of the 1st Assault Division (the X Reparto di Marcia), an experimental infantry 'T' (new Type) Battalion was set up, with four companies (each of the four platoons had automatic weapons like the experimental light machine guns and sub-machine guns), to test this new doctrinal innovation.

With the same goal in mind, the Reparti belonging to the Assault Army Corps were trained to march, sent to the front for a while, and held exercises with cavalry and light armoured units, which caused numerous complaints in the ranks. In fact, although maintaining the individual training and tactical concepts, the Assault Army Corps had wider-ranging tasks and was organised as a regular Army Corps, with supply, engineer and artillery units. The end of the war put paid to such experimentation and the Assault Army Corps was one of the first units to be disbanded.

Table 5.1: Reparto d'Assalto table of strength (May–August 1917)

Sub-unit	Officers	Troops	Machine guns	Sub-machine guns	Flame-throwers	Guns
HQ	3	36	2			
1st Assault Company	1					
1st Assault Platoon	1	42		2		
2nd Assault Platoon	1	42		2		
3rd Assault Platoon	1	42		2		
4th Assault Platoon	1	45		2		
1 Specialist Platoon		43	2			
Total	**5**	**214**	**2**	**8**		
2nd Assault Company	5	214	2	8		
3rd Assault Company	5	214	2	8		2
1 65mm-gun Section	1	37				
4th Assault Company (Replacement)	(5)	(214)	(2)	(8)		
1 Flame-thrower Section		27			15	
TOTAL	**19**	**715 (742)**	**6**	**24**	**(15)**	**2**

Table 5.2: Reparto d'Assalto table of strength (August 1918)

Sub-unit	Officers	Troops	Machine guns	Sub-machine guns	Flame-throwers	Guns
HQ	5	27				
1st Assault Company	1					
1st Assault Platoon	1	40				
2nd Assault Platoon	1	40				
3rd Assault Platoon	1	40				
4th Assault Platoon	1	40				
1st Submach. Section		24		6		
2nd Submach. Section		24		6		
Total	**5**	**208**		**12**		
2nd Assault Company	5	208		12		
3rd Assault Company	5	208		12		
1 MG Company	3	135	8			
3 Flame-thrower Sections	3	45			18	
1 Mortar Section	1	27				4
1 Supply Section		58				
TOTAL	**27**	**916**	**8**	**36**	**18**	**4**

AT WAR'S END

Demobilisation

The demobilisation process started immediately after the end of the war and by December 1918 fifteen classes (from 1874 to 1884) were discharged, while the discharge schedule of the other classes depended upon the country's internal situation (strikes and riots were commonplace) and international developments, in particular the increasing disputes with the new Kingdom of Slovenes, Croats and Serbs along Italy's eastern border regarding the possession of Dalmatia. In fact, the class of 1896 was not discharged until December 1919, when the class of 1900 was recalled, together with the class of 1901. A continuous process of redeployment was forced upon several units, who were called from the war zone to other parts of Italy to quell civil unrest, and most of the

Note: The Assault Army Corps had 12 Reparti d'Assalto (324 officers and 10,992 troops), plus 252 men (62 officers and 190 troops) in the various staffs (6 Assault Group HQs, 2 Regroupment HQs, 1 Machine Gun Group HQ) and 86 men (6 officers, 80 troops) in the two 37mm-gun units (4 × 37mm guns each) attached to each Regroupment, making a total of 11,654 Arditi (392 officers and 11,262 troops).

A Reparto parades in front of the Roman amphitheatre at Pola, in present-day Croatia. The Arditi units spearheaded the general Italian advance, and were the first units to enter many towns. (MGR 5/1942)

commands (one of them being the Assault Army Corps on 27 November 1918) and units were disbanded, on the basis of seniority.

An award of 500 lire, to be paid over five months, was granted to each soldier sent home directly from the unit. Italian prisoners coming from Austria were concentrated in camps where they were identified and interrogated, then, following leave, they were sent to a territorial unit while waiting for their class to be discharged. In the event of a unit being disbanded, the personnel not on the discharge list were transferred to other units, usually originating from the same mobilisation centre. In some instances troops had to move hundreds of kilometres, so as not to move their records from one depot to another one.

The Arditi units received the same treatment as other units. On 25 January 1919 all independent units and Reparti di Marcia were disbanded, and personnel not sent home were employed as replacements for the two existing divisions, or returned to their previous units. The two Reparti based in France were disbanded in March (XXXII) and July 1919 (II), due to France's decision to maintain a large part of its Army in service.

The end of war was an opportunity for senior officers who never liked the Arditi to show their true feelings, and surprisingly, they found Ten.Gen. (Gen.C.A.) Francesco Saverio Grazioli on their side. In fact, in a memorandum titled 'The possible destiny of Assault Troops', dated 18 November 1918, a few days after the end of the war, he sustained that the Arditi were only useful in wartime, and the possible employment of such troops during peacetime would be very dangerous, especially in tasks relating to public order, due to their way of thinking and acting, along with their trouble in maintaining proper discipline. In addition, he noted 'strange' and unauthorised relationships between extreme nationalist and futurist movements and some Arditi officers. He reasoned that the difference between the Arditi and regular infantry units was a only a matter of training, both military and physical, and that extending the training of such skills to regular infantry units was sufficient to maintain the innovations the Arditi represented. The right to bear the badge in future and the creation of a museum where standards, awards and memorabilia would be kept were adequate recognition for the Arditi. He also suggested that using them for colonial service would have been the perfect way to keep Arditi outside Italy during the demobilisation process, keeping them ready for an eventual deployment on the eastern border against Slavic threats.

Such logic was guided by the cold rationale of an Army officer rather than the sentiment of an Ardito. He had acted the same way when he organised the Assault Army Corps, trying to shape Ten.Col. Bassi's unusual and somewhat personal innovations into a regular instrument of war of the Italian Army.

The Supreme Command accepted Grazioli's suggestions and in March 1919 the 1st Assault Division was sent to Libya to start the operations of re-occupation, while the 2nd Assault Division was disbanded on 25 February and all personnel were either returned to their previous units or discharged.

In order to maintain a strategic reserve, an Inspectorate of Assault Troops was formed in May, with the task of organising territorial units of Arditi, drafting their personnel from among the discharged Arditi. In the words of the War Minister, Gen. Caviglia, the units were re-established with the aim of keeping the Arditi under control, while reinforcing their link with the Army and challenging any political exploitation of the veterans. All territorial units were disbanded in March 1920.

Back in Italy in June, after a ceasefire in Libya, the 1st Assault Division was deployed to the region of Emilia, but was soon moved to the eastern Italian border to face the renewed threats. While there, it was involved in the March on Fiume (12 September 1919). Headed by the famous poet, writer and war hero Gabriele D'Annunzio, a column of mutinying troops took over the town, and declared the Italian right to annex Fiume against the will of the Allied powers, influenced by the American president Wilson, and against the ineffective diplomatic efforts of the Italian government. The impact in Italy was enormous and

A group of Legionari Fiumani together with Arditi veterans. The uniform of the former was based on the Arditi one, although it was less heavy and of a lighter colour. The Legionari Fiumani badge was adopted in Fiume, with the motto '*Fiume o morte*' ('Fiume or death'). The Arditi, however, retained their own uniforms and badges. (Arch. Di Martino)

D'Annunzio with Arditi possibly from the XXII Reparto who, against orders, made their way to Fiume. They succeeded in capturing their unit's battle flag by means of a commando raid on their former comrades. (MGR 121/115)

many other veterans tried to reach Fiume, as well as many officers and soldiers who had deserted from their units. In particular, the whole VIII Reparto with its commander and the commander of the 3rd Assault Group, one company of the XII, some elements of the XIII, and one company of the XXII joined the rebels. The rest of the Division exhibited little hesitation in obeying orders. Nevertheless, the Chief of Staff prepared a plan to replace three Reparti with three Alpini battalions, but it was never completed, because on 10 January 1920 the Assault Division was disbanded.

Three Reparti d'Assalto (X, XX and XXII), the most loyal ones, were saved to form an Assault Regiment, together with a reconstituted IX Reparto under the command of Ten.Col. Messe, which was tasked with forming the replacement unit. The new IX Reparto took men from the territorial units. The assault regiment was sent to Albania in June and fought heavily at Valona, although the greatest losses were due to malaria. After returning to Italy in September, the last Reparti were definitively disbanded in December 1920.

AFTERMATH: THE ARDITO LEGACY IN THE 1920s

The creation and subsequent battlefield performance of the Arditi led to the impression that a new kind of Italian soldier had been born. This new image was exploited extensively in wartime propaganda, both internal and external to the Army. There was a strong need for the Army to show that a motivated soldier, confident in victory, still existed, especially after the defeat at Caporetto.

At the time, the official war propaganda proposed the heroic and abstract figure of a glorious soldier, inspired by mythical and classical literature, while public opinion and the media preferred the figure of the conscientious soldier, resigned to performing his duty while hating what he was doing, like the mountaineer Alpino or the peasant soldier.

For the Army, it was now possible to present the Ardito as a war-loving soldier, who fought to shorten the war, was dedicated to offensive action, and who cared little for the life of the enemy or for his own. These desired qualities offered a perfect representation of the new ideal within the Army during the reconstruction period following Caporetto: someone to trust in, someone who wanted revenge, and someone who was able to obtain victory.

It is important to note that the Arditi propaganda was partly created by the special 'VP' (Vigilance and Propaganda) offices instituted after

Caporetto to survey and influence the morale of the troops. However, it was mostly generated by the press and by public opinion, which were greatly influenced by the self-confidence that Arditi had shown and by magnifying wartime activities or everyday behaviour. Songs were the preferred and most immediate propaganda instruments. Black flames, hand grenades, daggers, death, black flags, hell, thunder and lightning were key words used: 'Where an Ardito is, there is a flag. No enemy will pass there'; 'The Ardito will attack with 25 grenades, and 25 grenades are 500 graves'; 'If you hear a song, open the door; the "Black Flames" are passing, going to their death'. A precious testimony can be found in some of Ernest Hemingway's works. The novelist, while he was an ambulance driver on the Italian front, wrote three poems, one being the famous 'Riparti d'Assalto': he also wrote a short story ('The disappearance of Pickles McCarty'), which was filled with admiration for the 'Black Flames' and for their contempt of death.

A portrait of Gabriele D'Annunzio in the uniform of an Ardito. On his cuff can be seen three promotion badges (two in silver and one in gold) and his rank insignia (Tenente Colonnello). On his left sleeve is the Ardito's badge (the Fiume version) and aviation wings. The cap badge is of the cavalry (lancer's) type, with the propeller reserved for aviation troops, indicating the units with which the poet served during the war. On his lapel there is an impressive array of decorations, including the Military Order of Savoy, and one Gold, two Silver and two Bronze Valour Medals. (MGR 134/145)

The hard training, dress distinctions and the institution of a special badge, together with particular privileges and benefits, allowed the Arditi to consider themselves an elite force, and the relaxed discipline was considered an award for the higher risk faced in battle. The self-proclamation of their successes and sacrifices, the boasting of their conduct which was frequently beyond the rules of the Army, the camaraderie and their sometimes excessive *esprit de corps* became the origin of a particular way of acting and thinking, labelled 'Arditism'. This ideological belief held by all Arditi was immortalised after the war in several memoirs written by Arditi officers. These greatly exaggerated the role the Arditi played in wartime operations, especially when other infantry units were involved; they delighted in reporting all manner of infringments of military and civil law whether minor or severe, and exalted the Ardito's way of solving problems, with a dagger and hand grenades. The existence of this feeling of being above the law, while being authorised to remain there, pushed many Arditi veterans toward some of the extremist and nationalist movements that manifested themselves at the end of the war.

The first such associations were developed by Futurist thinkers who had also been Arditi, like Mario Carli in Rome and Ferruccio Vecchi in Milan. On 18 September 1918, in the Futurist journal *Roma Futurista* Carli wrote: 'Now we have a mission. Italy created her Arditi to be saved from all enemies ... Our dagger serves to kill all internal and external monsters, which threaten our Country ... The Arditi are the real vanguard of the nation'. In October Filippo Tommaso Marinetti, one of the most important Futurist figures, gave a number of speeches to Arditi officers:

You are the first, the best, the most deserving soldiers. You are the future owners of Italy. I love your insolent impudence. You have every right, when you slaughter an Austrian soldier ... You are not only the best Italian soldiers ... You are the new Italian generation, fearless and brilliant, that will prepare the great future for Italy!

On 1 January 1919 Mario Carli founded the Association of Italian Arditi in Rome and on 19 January the Milan section began to operate under the control of Ferruccio Vecchi. The Milan section, whose seat was Marinetti's home, would become the most important, even though it had fewer members, due to the proximity to another extremist movement then on the rise: Fascism. Connections between Mussolini and the Arditi's Association became so strong that armed Arditi served as guards at the entrance of Mussolini's newspaper offices, *Il Popolo d'Italia*, and many Arditi were founders of the *Fasci di Combattimento* in Piazza San Sepolcro in Milan on 23 March 1919.

On 15 April a group of 40 Arditi, under the command of Vecchi and inspired by Mussolini, attacked a group of striking Socialists in the centre of Milan with revolvers and hand grenades. They also attacked, ransacked and burnt the offices of the socialist newspaper *L'Avanti!* This was the only organised raid conducted by Arditi, who in the following months swelled the ranks of the intervention squads of Fascist paramilitary units (a phenomenon called *squadrismo*), employed in the suppression of socialist and proletarian riots and strikes.

The growing Fascist movement, which was better organised and funded, checked the expansion of the Arditi Association, which entered into the sphere of the D'Annunzian movement, a less political but no less nationalistic movement headed by Gabriele D'Annunzio. In fact, during the Fiume affair, the Arditi Association looked to D'Annunzio as the new leader, and subscribed to many of the statements of the poet, who was named its honorary president.

The feeling fostered by the Arditi for D'Annunzio was fully reciprocated by the poet, since about one-third of all mutinied troops had been Arditi, and he adopted a version of the Ardito's badge, for his Legionari. He himself began to dress as an Ardito and to use mottoes and ceremonies typical of the assault troops. In the rest of the country, Futurists, nationalists and Arditi organised demonstrations and rallies and influenced public opinion through enthusiastic newspaper articles, in the hope of a coup. The inglorious and tragic end to the

A propaganda postcard issued after the war, aimed at consolidating the image of the Ardito as an audacious soldier – the first to take on the enemy trenches armed with the distinctive dagger and hand grenade.
(Arch. Ufficio Storico FNAI)

Arditi troops from Rome present a standard to D'Annunzio, which is dedicated to their Arditi comrades in Fiume. The Tenente on the right is a 'Crimson Flame' (note the cap badge and the collar patches), while the standard-bearer is an Aiutante di Battaglia (the highest NCO rank) who sports three wound badges on his right sleeve. The black armband on the Ardito to the right of D'Annunzio indicates that he had two relatives die during the war. (Coll. Franco Mesturini)

Fiume occupation, on 5 January 1921, under the attack and shelling of regular Italian troops, witnessed the decline of support for D'Annunzio's movement in favour of the Fascists.

Meanwhile, a new fascist-sponsored National Association of Italian Arditi (ANAI) was founded from the remnants of the Milan section, with its members linked to Mussolini. With Fascist help, the ANAI soon had more than 100 sections all over Italy, many of which were strictly related to the local section of the Fascist party.

Many leaders of the ANAI saw the return of D'Annunzio to the Association in April 1922 as a way of gaining independence from the Fascist movement, and agreed again to a platform based on D'Annunzio's nationalistic program. In reaction to this move, Mussolini sponsored a new Federation of Italian Arditi (FNAI), and many of the best-known commanders, including Col. Bassi and Magg. Freguglia, were co-opted into the leadership. The official foundation of the FNAI occurred on 23 October 1922, five days before the 'March on Rome', which began the Fascist rise to power.

For the next two years, the FNAI sections took up all ANAI sections, and when a merger was not possible, the Fascist authorities dissolved the non-orthodox sections. It is important to remember that a leftist association did exist, created from the Rome section of the ANAI. The *Arditi del Popolo* (The People's Arditi) gathered anarchic and republican Arditi from all over Italy, but failed to represent a valid socialist alternative to the ANAI, largely because it was considered to be a provocation by leftist parties. This movement was active in 1921 for three to four months.

In the 1930s, the FNAI co-operated with the Fascist regime's propaganda machine, stressing the links between wartime valour and Fascist *squadrismo* while keeping alive the memoirs of the actions in the war. On the other hand, Fascism adopted many of the Arditi's practices to give the regime's ceremonies a martial aspect, and to underline their common origins. The cry 'To whom the honour? To us!' was taken from the traditions of the Arditi, the skull with the dagger clenched between the teeth became the standard symbol of *squadrismo*, the Arditi badge itself became the collar patch pin in the years of the Italian Social Republic (RSI), and one of the most renowned Fascist songs, '*Giovinezza*' (Youthfulness), had also belonged to the Arditi.

MUSEUMS, COLLECTIONS AND ASSOCIATIONS

Many museums in Italy have features on World War I, but only a few have specific material on the Arditi. If we leave out the three main museums of the *Risorgimento* (Rome, Milan and Turin), where World War I is considered as the last war for the unity of Italy, the only museum specifically dedicated to World War I and scientifically organised is the *Museo Storico Italiano della Guerra* in Rovereto, Trento (www.museodellaguerra.it). In its precious collection is a complete Ardito's uniform, a wide collection of weapons and hand grenades used by assault troops, and a library containing around 40,000 photographs and 20,000 volumes.

Some uniforms and memoirs of the Arditi are located in the *Museo Storico Militare* in Palmanova (Udine), and in the *Piccolo Museo Roberto Favero* museum, in Solagna (Vicenza).

A source for research on weapons is the *Museo Nazionale dell'Artiglieria* (www.esercito.difesa.it/musei/museo_artiglieria.as p) in Turin, which has the biggest collection of Italian Army weapons.

The Arditi's lorries can be seen at the *Museo Memoriale della Libertà*, in Bologna S.Lazzaro (www.museomemoriale.com) and at the *Museo Storico della Motorizzazione Militare* (www.esercito.difesa.it/musei/museo _motorizzazione.asp) in Rome-Cecchignola.

As far as the author is aware, only two groups of World War I re-enactors exist in Italy, one being the '*Sentinelle del Lagazuoi*' (http://utenti.tripod.it/sentinelle), and one dedicated to Arditi, the '*Guerrieri per gioco*' (www.jollyrogerxxx.it).

Two veterans associations exist, the *Associazione Nazionale Incursori Esercito* (http://members.xoom.virgilio.it/ANIE/) and the *Federazione Nazionale Arditi d'Italia*, the successor to the FNAI founded in 1922, obviously without any political affiliation. The Turin section manages the historical archives (www.arpnet.it/arditi).

GLOSSARY

Alpino (pl. **Alpini**) A mountain soldier (the name comes from the Alps). He wears a special hat with crow's feathers, and green flames as collar patches.

Ardito (pl. **Arditi**) A member of an Assault unit, trained and equipped as a stormtrooper. Also known as a 'Black Flame' (the colour of his collar patches).

Ardito Reggimentale (pl. **Arditi Reggimentali**) A soldier of a special platoon at regimental level in the regular infantry units, trained and equipped as an Ardito.

Bersagliere (pl. **Bersaglieri**) Literally a 'sharpshooter', a member of a light infantry unit, sometimes equipped with bicycles (Bersaglieri Ciclisti). They are famous for running instead of marching, and for their cockerel-feathered hat or helmet. They wore crimson flames as collar patches.

Carabiniere (pl. **Carabinieri**) A member of the Italian Military Police, organised on the model of the Gendarmerie in France. Their name comes from the carabina (carbine), the rifle in use.

Esploratore (pl. **Esploratori**) Special soldiers akin to scouts recruited and trained by the Italian Army from 1914, and organised at regimental level.

Legionario (pl. **Legionari**) A volunteer in the 1919 March on Fiume. The name derives from the Latin military term.

Moschetto '91 Literally a 'musket'; a carbine version of the Italian standard rifle.

Mostrine Collar patches.

Nonno Literally, a 'grandfather'; an Arditi veteran.

Pugnale d'assalto A dagger, the archetypal weapon of the Arditi: several types were in use.

Reparto d'Assalto (pl. **Reparti d'Assalto**) A battalion-sized assault unit.

Reparto d'Assalto di Marcia Replacement Assault Unit.

SIPE A type of hand grenade, common to the regular army, but not used by the Arditi.

Thevenot Another type of hand grenade, used by the Arditi.

BIBLIOGRAPHY

'Nel XVII annuale della costituzione della Sezione di Milano', *L'Ardito d'Italia* (Milan, 1936)

Aponte, S. *L'avanguardia del Grappa. Il IX Reparto d'Assalto Fiamme Nere* (Rome, 1921)

Baccio, B. 'La grande falange d'assalto', *La Lettura* n.5, pp. 685–696 (Milan, Oct. 1918)

Baseggio, C. *La Compagnia Arditi Baseggio 1915–1916* (Milan, 1923)

Baseggio, C. *La Compagnia della Morte* (Venice, 1929)

Bertè, T. *Il colpo di mano italiano alla Foraora* (Rovereto, 1998)

Brambilla, A. and Fossati, I. *Medaglie a Croce FFAA – Italian Cross Medals 1900–1989* (Milan, 1993)

Businelli, A. Gli *Arditi del IX* (Rome, 1934)

Calamandrei, C. *Storia dell'arma bianca italiana da Waterloo al nuovo millennio* (Florence, 1999)

Carli, M. *L'Arditismo* (Rome/Milan, 1929)

Carli, M. *Noi Arditi* (Milan, 1919)

Corsaro, G. *Arditi in guerra* (Milan, 1935)

Del Giudice, E. and V. *Uniformi militari italiane dal 1861 ai giorni nostri* (Milan, 1968)

Drury, I. *German Stormtrooper 1914–18*, Osprey Warrior series No. 12 (Oxford, 1995)

Fabi, L. *Musei della Grande Guerra, Guida* (Trento, 2001)

Farina, S. *Le truppe d'assalto italiane* (Rome, 1938)

Fatutta, F. 'Contributo ad una storia delle Truppe d'Assalto', *Studi Storico Militari 2000* (Ufficio Storico SME)

Fatutta, F. 'L'epopea degli Arditi', *Rivista Italiana Difesa* 12/91, pp. 90–97

Freguglia, L. (ed.) *XXVII Battaglione d'Assalto. Monte Piana, Montello, Vittorio Veneto* (Milan, 1937)

Gallinari, V. *L'Esercito italiano nel primo dopoguerra* (Rome, 1980)

Giudici, P. *Fiamme Nere. Note di Gloria e di Passione* (Florence, 1920)

Giudici, P. *Reparti d'Assalto* (Milan, 1928)

Giuliani, R. *Gli Arditi: breve storia dei reparti d'assalto della IIIa Armata* (Milan, 1919)

Gudmundson, B.I. *Stormtroop tactics. Innovation in the German Army, 1914–1918* (Westport, 1989)

Longo, L.E. *Francesco Saverio Grazioli* (Rome, 1989)

Longo, L.E. *L'Esercito Italiano e la questione Fiumana* (Rome 1996)

Mantoan, N. *Armi ed equipaggiamenti dell'Esercito Italiano nella Grande Guerra 1915–18* (Noale, 1996)

Mantoan, N. *Bombe a mano italiane 1915–1918* (Udine, 2000)

Massignani, A. *Le truppe d'assalto austroungariche nella Grande Guerra* (Noale, 1995)

Menichetti, A. 'I distintivi degli Arditi', *Uniformi ed Armi* No. 11 (1990), pp. 20–25

Mesturini, F. and Lazzarini, F. 'Gli Arditi dei Reparti d'Assalto', *Uniformi ed Armi* No. 57 (1995), pp. 6–18

Montanari, M. *Politica e Strategia in Cent'anni di Guerre Italiane*, Vol. 2, T. 2 (Rome, 2000)

Nicolle, D. and Ruggeri, R. *The Italian Army of World War I*, Osprey Men-at-Arms series No. 387 (Oxford, 2003)

Palieri, M. *Gli Arditi. Gloria e sacrifizi degli assaltatori* (Milan, 1932)

Pettinelli, R.F. *Armi portatili e munizioni militari italiane 1870–1998.* (Udine, 2002)

Radicati di Primeglio, M. *I Reparti d'Assalto della Guerra 1915–18* (Turin, 1957)

Rochat, G. 'I Reparti d'Assalto esistenti al 15 giugno 1918', *Memorie Storiche Militari 1982*, pp.515–520

Rochat, G. *Gli Arditi della Grande Guerra. Origini, Battaglie, Miti*, 2nd (revised) edition (Gorizia, 1990)

Simone, G. Belogi, R. and Grimaldi, A. *Il 91* (Milan, 1970)

Stefani, F. *La Storia della Dottrina e degli Ordinamenti dell'Esercito Italiano*, Vol. 2, T. 1 (Rome, 1985)

Tenente Anonimo, *Arditi in guerra* (Milan, 1934)

Tenente Anonimo, *Glorie e miserie della trincea* (Milan, 1933)

Ufficio Storico Stato Maggiore Esercito, *Le Grandi Unità nella Guerra Italo-Austriaca*, 2 vols (Rome, 1926)

Ufficio Storico Stato Maggiore Esercito, *L'Esercito Italiano nella Grande Guerra*, 7 vols. 37 tomes (Rome, 1940–89), in particular Vol. V, T. 1, 1 bis, 1ter; Vol. V, T. 2, 2 bis, 2 ter; Vol. VI, T .2.

Viotti, A. *L'uniforme in grigio verde (1909–19)* (Rome, 1994)

Zoppi, O. *Due volte con gli Arditi sul Piave* (Bologna, 1938)

COLOUR PLATE COMMENTARY

A: ARDITI CORPORAL (CAPORAL MAGGIORE)

The corporal (A) wears the first-pattern combat uniform designed by Ten.Col. Bassi, with the open tunic, black-flame collar patches (1a), a green turtleneck sweater and Alpini-style trousers, with puttees and Alpini-style hobnailed boots (1b). On his left sleeve he wears the Ardito's badge (2), while on his right sleeve he has a 'twice-wounded' badge in silver (3). On his cuffs, over the rank stripes in black woollen yarn, he also bears a war-promotion badge in silver yarn (4).

His mod.16 helmet has the Ardito's badge stencilled on, and a raised chinstrap so as not to interfere with wearing his gas mask. The issue dagger, in its leather scabbard, and the two twin-cartridge pouches are on his belt. Each pouch, in grey-green leather as per the 1915 regulations, contains 24 x 6.5mm cartridges (5), assembled in four six-round magazines (6). Between 12 and 15 'Thevenot' hand grenades (7) are carried in the hand-grenade sack (the haversack mod.1907/09) along with a canteen mod.1907, in poplar or willow wood, strapped on. The rifle is the Moschetto '91 mod. Cavalleria (cavalry carbine), the standard Ardito weapon.

Other details shown are: (8) an Ardito's dagger. Notches engraved on the handle, according to memoirs, represented a sustained assault, or a kill. (9) The carbine's muzzle, with opened-out bayonet, and (10) a cutaway of its loading mechanism. (11) The *Petardo Offensivo* (P.O.), an 'offensive hand grenade' used by the Arditi. (12) The Italian *Polivalente* gas mask, and its tin box (13): the inscription reads 'He who takes off his mask, dies. Always keep it with you.' (14) Identity tags. (15) This inset shows the changes to the uniform made after Caporetto: the grey-green shirt and black tie have been adopted in favour of the sweater, and the figure wears the black fez as headgear.

B: A 'DEATH COMPANY' ATTACK, THE CARSO PLAINS, OCTOBER 1915

Due to the state of entrenchment along the whole front, specialist soldiers, organised in Wire-cutter companies (also known as 'Death' companies), were tasked with the dangerous job of dealing with enemy barbed wire. These troops wore Farina body armour, comprising a steel helmet weighing 2.2/2.8kg with an armoured frontal plate and a 30×40cm breastplate made up of seven 1mm-thick steel plates that weighed 8.6kg. They carried wire-cutting tools and explosives.

The lance-corporal (1) has a pocket wire-cutter in one hand and is armed with the long mod.'91 rifle. The latter mounts a wire-cutting mechanism on the muzzle, which aligns the wire with the breech and allows it to be shot through with a bullet, thus severing it. He has the Esploratore badge on his left sleeve.

His companion (2) is using the larger 'squad' wire-cutters and wears rubberised gloves as protection against electrified wire. The engineer (3) waits for the opening to be made (engineers could be recognised by their black, crimson-edged collar patches): he will then place gelatin tubes under the wire, which will then blow a bigger opening. He is taking shelter behind a Masera trench shield. On the ground next to him lies a long 'Malfatti' wire-cutting device: the wire was hooked on the end, and pulled sharply backwards, thus severing it.

C: ARDITI TRAINING SCHOOL, SDRICCA DI MANZANO, 1917

The date is September 1917, and new candidates have just arrived at Sdricca di Manzano. To test their mental strength and reactions under stress, the candidates had Thevenot hand grenades thrown at them by the so-called 'grandfathers' (those who have already passed the course).

The candidates have been given the Ardito's tunic: however, they are not allowed to wear the black-flame collar patches nor the badge, so they still wear their regimental collar patches, in this case the bicolour patches of the 239th Infantry Regiment, Pesaro Brigade, of the 59th Division, 8th Army Corps, 2nd Army. The previous selection process seems to have been done according to plan; indeed, one of the candidates sports the 'VE' valour badge, indicating he has already volunteered for several risky operations.

In the background, a mock enemy hill is under attack by other Arditi already in training, with direct (live) fire coming from a 65mm gun and a Fiat 14 machine gun. This was the final test before the trainees could be considered combat-ready Arditi.

D: CAPTAIN (CAPITANO), XXIX REPARTO

This captain (A) of XXIX Reparto, promoted for war merit, wears the standard uniform with the open tunic and the green-flame collar patches, the grey-green shirt with black tie, and the Alpini-style trousers. He has woollen socks and the Alpini-style boots. Three Reparti (III, XXIX and LII) and one company of VI, XXX and IV and the XI Reparto di Marcia, manned by Alpini, used to wear the green flames and Alpini-style felt hats.

The Alpino hat shown (1) is the mod.1909 with the Ardito badge (2), which also has the designation of the unit in Roman numerals. The Ardito's cap badge originated from the Bersaglieri's, but with left-pointing flames and crossed Roman swords instead of rifles. On the hat, the three stripes identify his rank. For camouflage purposes, the standard eagle feather has been removed from the hat.

He has been awarded a Military Valour Cross (3), and has two years of war service, as indicated by the two bronze stars on the ribbon of his 1915–18 campaign medal (4). He is armed with a captured Austro-Hungarian *Sturmmesser* dagger and with the Glisenti (mod.1910) automatic pistol in its leather holster (5), attached to a 'Sam Browne' belt (non-standard, but common in 1918). The Glisenti was called the 'poor-man's Luger' due to its appearance and frequent glitches: loading it with the original Luger 9mm ammunition was dangerous, as this was too powerful. The captain is resting on a long pickaxe.

Other details shown are: (6) the Ardito officer's badge, with oak leaves sewn in gold thread. (7) The Bodeo revolver (mod.1889 B), with trigger guard: this was reserved for officers only. (8) The officer's war promotion badge, with crossed swords: for promotions up to captain it was in silver, up to colonel it was in gold, and up to general it was in gold on red backing. (9) The Arditi Cross was issued by the FNAI in the early 1920s, recalling the symbols of the assault units, namely skull and dagger. (10) A rare commemorative medal issued by XXX Reparto, with the classic skull and dagger symbols and, on the verso (11), a list of the battles fought by the unit (with thanks to the *coll.* Andrea Brambilla).